PL 94-142

An Act of Congress

PL 94-142
An Act of Congress

Erwin L. Levine
Department of Government
Skidmore College
Saratoga Springs, N.Y.

Elizabeth M. Wexler
Associate Director
Federal State Relations
Council of Chief State School Officers
Washington, D.C.

Macmillan Publishing Co., Inc.
NEW YORK

Collier Macmillan Publishers
LONDON

Macmillan Publishing Co., Inc.
866 Third Avenue, New York, New York 10022

Collier Macmillan Canada, Ltd.

Library of Congress Cataloging in Publication Data

Levine, Erwin L.
　　PL 94-142: An act of Congress.

　　Includes index.
　　1. United States. Law, statutes, etc. Education
for all handicapped children act. 2. Handicapped
children—Education—Law and legislation—United States.
I. Wexler, Elizabeth M., joint author. II. Title.
KF4210.A314A164　　　344.73'0791　　　80-18071
ISBN　0-02-370270-2

Printing: 1 2 3 4 5 6 7 8　　Year: 1 2 3 4 5 6 7 8

For Adam
Whose youthful innocence will grow into compassion and understanding.

E. W.

Preface

Every student of politics knows that the passage of a bill through Congress is a very complicated process. Most legislation starts as an idea in someone's or some group's mind and is then processed through a maze of administrative and congressional people. Original responsibility for pointing out the need for specific legislation may rest with a national, regional or local interest group, a Senate or House staffer, a professional administrator in a federal or state agency, an elected official, or someone close to one of the above. Regardless of its parentage, a bill does not become a law easily. Circumstances have to be right, various interests must intersect at exactly the right moment, and a concurrency among the principal actors in the legislative process must somehow be reached. The American system of government, with its federal and separation of powers principles and the bicameral nature of the Congress, does not make for easy sledding, no matter how "right" the bill might be.

It took ten years for the *Education For All Handicapped Children Act of 1975* (Public Law 94–142) to be enacted. Interest groups for handicapped children and sympathetic members of the Congress and their staffs plotted and maneuvered through a decade to secure into federal law the principle that all handicapped, just as non-handicapped, children were entitled to a free appropriate public education. Not only were they successful in printing that principle in the permanency of a specific Act of Congress, but they also wrote into the law procedural safeguards and guidelines to bring state and local education agencies into compliance with the new standards.

But once a bill becomes a law, its "bare bones" must be "fleshed out" by the federal agency empowered to administer the law. Within the process of writing the regulations which give a law "its life," another political process takes place, involving the same "actors" who had a vital role and interest in the original passage of the law. To administer the regulations takes funding by successive Congresses. Those people interested in keeping the law viable and useful must be constantly aware of the need to press the Congress and the Executive branch for continuous commitment to the cause.

Only by following a bill from its inception as an idea to the implementation of its provisions after it has been enacted into law, can the student of politics learn about most of the important aspects of the creation and implementation of an Act of Congress. PL 94-142 lends itself to that understanding.

E. L. L.
E. M. W.

Contents

Contents

Contents

PL 94-142

An Act of Congress

1

Introduction

The Constitution and the Political Process

The American political system is grounded in two constitu-
tionally-rooted principles: the separation of powers and
federalism. The former delineates, albeit imperfectly,
authority and power among the three traditional branches of
government — legislative, executive and judicial — while the
latter divides authority and power between the national and
state governments. Boundary lines among the branches and
between the two sovereignties of nation and state are blurred
at best. In order to "get things done," the legislative and
executive branches are forced to cooperate to overcome the
separate but shared powers that keep them apart. This coop-
erative effort, sometimes more enthusiastic on the part of
one than the other, must be within constitutional limitations
as interpreted by the judiciary with its immense power of
judicial review. For a bill to become a law, the Congress must
come into agreement with the President (or override his
veto). And, for the law to have the effect that the Congress
intended, it must be administered by the Executive branch
within the broad outlines as written by the Congress. Much

leeway is given the executive, once the law goes "on the books," to carry out the intent of the Congress.

The federal principle forces the states to contend with each other through their Senators and Representatives in the Congress, and, if the law is of the domestic variety, brings the national government and the states into a partnership. The states are often the vehicles for administering much domestic policy as outlined by the Congress and the recipients of federal appropriations. The national (or federal) government becomes the enforcer of federal law, but when the law establishes rules and regulations which the states are bound to follow under federal law, the partnership can become uneasy and tenuous.

An excellent example of the application of the principle of separation of powers and federalism to the realm of political practice can be found in Public Law 94–142, the Education for All Handicapped Children Act, which was signed into law by President Gerald Ford on November 29, 1975. We can gain much insight into the American political system by examining not only the process by which the legislation came into being, but also the politics of administering the law after its enactment by the 94th Congress. The Act lends itself to a fuller appreciation of the intricacies of how a bill becomes a law and how that law is enforced, because of the circumstances surrounding this type of legislation. One would think that once Congress recognized the difficulties encountered by physically and mentally handicapped children (and their families) in securing an appropriate education, it would act swiftly and decisively to ensure that handicapped children received what is their due, that it would supply the states the financial means for the excess costs required to educate such handicapped children. But that was not the case, because the politics of obtaining legislation favorable to a cause must be adapted to the political system. Constitutional delineation of power and authority dictates to a remarkable degree the procedures any group must adopt to move the Congress to turn recognition of a problem into an Act of Congress written to solve the problem.

As finally enacted in 1975, PL 94-142 was to assure that all handicapped children had available to them a "free appropriate public education" that emphasized special education and related services designed to meet their needs. In addition, the Act was an attempt to assure that the rights of handicapped children and their parents or guardians were protected; to assist state and local government to provide for the education of handicapped children; and, to assess and assure the effectiveness of efforts to educate handicapped children. PL 94-142 secured in federal law what handicapped children and their parents had been seeking: enforcement of the right to an education and the supplying of federal funds to ensure it. The Education for all Handicapped Children Act is comprehensive, and we shall not outline its various provisions here. Suffice it for now to point out why PL 94-142 is worth examining for an understanding of American politics and the role of legislation in our lives.

1. Interest Group activity. Congress cannot function without interest groups which provide information, stimulus and support. The groups that advocated a greater federal role in the education of handicapped children were in the forefront throughout the period of urging Congress to act. They continued to be vitally important in the formulation of the rules as laid down by the Department of Health, Education and Welfare through the Office of Education after passage of PL 94-142.

2. Timing. Federal aid for educating handicapped children did not happen overnight. It took about a decade for Congress to put together a comprehensive legislative program for handicapped children. Congress responded to the needs of handicapped children in a piecemeal fashion and only after a great deal of pressure from the handicapped constituency had been brought to bear on it.

3. Congressional Procedures. A bicameral or two-house system makes for duplication of efforts on the part of those interested in specific legislation. In addition, the committee and subcommittee system are the hub around which the process in Congress revolves. The composition of committees and subcommittees and the role of their staff are extremely important in the success rate of legislation. In PL 94–142 we can see the interplay between the staff of the committees, the interest groups, and the executive agencies — the so-called "iron triangle" — as handicapped legislation slowly made its way to law.

4. Presidential Leadership. We are accustomed to think that no really important legislation can be enacted without strong presidential support. This was not the case with PL 94–142. Although Presidents Kennedy and Johnson lent their office and influence in urging handicapped legislation, Nixon and Ford did not. PL 94–142 came into being despite Nixon and Ford, and not because of them.

5. Creation of a Federal Agency. When Congress creates something that must be administered, either it empowers an established Department or Agency to carry out the provisions of the law or it creates a new federal entity. In the case of PL 94–142, the Congress made permanent that which it had earlier made temporary, the Bureau of Education for the Handicapped (BEH), in order to fill a void in HEW.[1] Further-

---

[1] In 1979, the Congress created a separate Department of Education. The BEH then became part of the new department. Throughout this work, however, we shall refer to the BEH as part of the Department of Health, Education and Welfare for the sake of historical accuracy.

more, in building the BEH into a powerful office, the Congress took an active lead in legislating political muscle for BEH, going so far as to protect the Director of BEH by covering him with the mantle of Civil Service. In doing this, the Congress responded directly to the requests of the handicapped interest groups to have their own advocate in the federal executive structure.

6. *The Federal Regulations.* When Congress writes a law, and designates an executive body to carry it out, the regulations (or "regs") to administer the law must be written *after* passage of the law. How the "regs" are written and what they do are also subject to scrutiny by the interest groups. In PL 94-142 the interest groups for the handicapped had a very important role to play to ensure that the "regs" were written in the most advantageous way for them.

7. *The Judiciary.* The aims of the handicapped interest groups were two-fold. First, they attempted to have Congress legislate their needs and requirements. Second, they used the courts and litigation as a means of advancing their cause. The purpose was to bring the judiciary to the point of recognizing that a free, appropriate public education was indeed a constitutional right, not just a privilege subject to state whim. In this they succeeded by taking a page out of the battle for civil rights by the NAACP. Once the courts had ruled in favor of civil rights, they had added political arguments to write the "civil rights" of the handicapped into PL 94-142.

8. *Federal-State Relationship.* When the Congress enacts a federal law which requires state action, there is always the difficulty of enforcement, let alone enticement of the states to take part in the administering of the law. Enticement usually takes the form of using federal funds as "bait" in either a direct grant or a grant-in-aid system. Once a state

agrees to take part in the process, as outlined by the federal law, the state is fairly well bound to carry out its obligations. But differences of opinion as to how the law should be interpreted by the state, as opposed to the interpretation placed on the law by the federal agency, are certain to rise. In the case of educating handicapped children, the states were not the primary force urging the Congress to act. That role was in the hands of the interest groups representing the handicapped. The states came onto the scene later, a couple of years prior to the passage of PL 94-142. Although the states wanted the financial support of the federal government, they did not want stringent federal requirements, which PL 94-142 did indeed have. States fear encroachment on their "turf" and at times make it very difficult for the federal government to enforce what is intended to be national policy — in this case educating handicapped children. Currently a form of "tug-of-war" does exist between the federal government and many of the states as to the enforcement of PL 94-142.

9. Oversight. The Congressional role does not stop with enactment of the law and establishment of an executive agency to administer the law. The authorization of funds by the Act of Congress establishes only a ceiling on the amount of money that is to be spent, not a floor. The appropriations process is a separate one, and it is there that success of the program might be undercut by short-changing. Furthermore, authorization and appropriations are only for a set number of years, and then Congress must re-examine the situation to determine whether the law should be changed, or whether funds should be redistributed in a different manner with an altered set of priorities. It is here, in the function of oversight, that the "iron triangle" once more comes into play, and it is here that the states can express to the Congress, through the committees holding oversight hearings, what they think about the efficacy of the law. The record is put in the public eye through oversight hearings, and out of the oversight hearings come new recommendations from the interest groups, the executive branch, and the committees themselves. In the case of educating handicapped children, the oversight hearings, held to determine how effective each step had been, eventually led to Public Law 94-142, which itself would be subject to new oversight hearings as well.

THE FEDERAL ROLE IN EDUCATION

Most Americans take it for granted that public education at the elementary and secondary levels is not only a requirement mandated by state and local government but it is part of our national heritage. Without widespread public education, there can be no educated electorate, and without an educated electorate, there can be no viable democracy. Education is our birthright; it is owed to us in order that we may be able to make a living, grow intellectually, and govern ourselves. In a word, so that we may be a free people. Contrary to popular belief, however, a free public education is guaranteed by state, not federal, constitutions.

Education is the business of the states. Provisions for educating our children were not made in the United States Constitution, because, in the early years of the nation, no one thought the federal government was supposed to play a role in the development of educational systems for the nation's children and youth. The 10th Amendment to the Constitution implies that education is one of those areas outside the purview of the national government and thus reserved to the states. State sovereignty means that the states police themselves and provide for their own internal governance. The national government was to be responsible for external affairs and for those few things related to the passage of commerce between and among the states. Our children and youth, therefore, are due a public education, not by reason of a Constitution of the United States, but because of provisions in state Constitutions, state law, and tradition. How, then, did the federal government get into the education business on such a large scale?

In the face of widespread unrest during the 1960's, the American people came to believe that the solution to national problems could be found by the national government. Groups within the society concerned about civil rights, poverty, employment, and housing perceived education as one sure way to begin addressing their special needs. Education was the first step on the ladder to self-improvement in an upwardly mobile society. In order for education to fulfill these expectations, it had to be free and unsegregated, and maintain high standards of quality as well.

Congress and the President listened not only to the appeals of those special interest groups but also to state and local education officials who argued that their limited resources could not finance these added burdens in addition to general education services. Two pieces of legislation stand out as the federal government's response to these demands. Titles IV and VI of the Civil Rights Act of 1964 prohibited discrimination in any program receiving federal assistance on the basis of race, color, or national origin and provided assistance to state and local education agencies to carry out desegregation of the public schools. Then, in 1965, the Congress passed PL 89-10, the Elementary and Secondary Education Act of 1965, which included programs for compensatory education for low-income students, for libraries, for educational innovation and for strengthening state and local education agencies. Accountability was to be assured by restrictions on the use of these federal funds.

When the federal government supplies *any* money, along with it comes some form of federal regulation, requirements, and reporting of the results derived from the use of the federal money. The states share the financial burden in varying degrees, depending upon the specific program. No matter how low the percentage of the federal contribution, however, the program must adhere to federal standards.

The states, therefore, enter into a partnership with the federal government, from which it is difficult to withdraw even if they want to. Since 1965, when the Congress passed The Elementary and Secondary Education Act (ESEA) in the spirit of President Lyndon Johnson's War on Poverty, the federal role in education has become a fact of life. A contractual relationship that has been formed between state and federal governments is not likely to diminish. The acceptance of the federal government as a partner in education has facilitated its entrance into almost every aspect of education through the requirements it places on the recipients of its funds. In this manner, the federal government runs education assistance programs in all the states which in fiscal year 1980 lay claim to upwards of $12 billion in the Department of Health, Education and Welfare alone.

One of the groups with special needs that has benefited by increased federal involvement in education is the handicapped. Since 1966, when ESEA was amended to include programs for handicapped children, the rights of the handicapped have been pursued vigorously in the courts and in the legislatures on every level by parents, teachers and civil rights organizations. The following chapters trace the development of federal special education laws through the activities of these groups until the enactment of PL 94-142, the Education for All Handicapped Children Act of 1975. This legislation is considered landmark legislation because it centralizes education programs for handicapped children in the federal office (BEH) and thus makes official federal responsibility in educating handicapped children. It also establishes that a free appropriate public education is a federally prescribed right to which handicapped children are entitled.

We shall look at how the process of politics drew the federal and state governments together in a bid to provide a public individualized education for the nation's handicapped children and youth. This book is a story of the creation of a public law and its implementation. An Act of Congress legitimizes the intent of Congress. But that intent must be written into and translated by administrative rules and regulations in the executive branches of both the federal and state governments. We shall examine what role they have to play in implementing the intent of the law.

2

Building the Case for Educating Handicapped Children

An interest group is any collection of people organized to promote some common objective that somehow relates to the political process.[1] An interest group (or pressure group), in a political sense, is composed of people with like-minded interests who are represented by their own members or by a professional staff in the corridors of executive and legislative halls. We are a pluralistic society consisting of thousands of overlapping and intersecting groups of many different interests. These groups involve themselves in the political process because they feel they must protect themselves against what they deem "poor legislation" that will deprive them of "something" or to obtain passage of "good legislation" that will give them "something." They must therefore become deeply involved in politics at both national and state levels.

The problems of handicapped children, particularly related to securing an adequate education, represent a phenomenon which had its roots in the civil rights movements

[1] Erwin L. Levine and Elmer E. Cornwell, Jr., *An Introduction to American Government*, 4th ed. (New York: Macmillan, 1979), 68.

of the 1960's. In that decade many Blacks believed they were getting less than they were entitled to in education, employment, housing and accommodations and came together to obtain their rights. They confronted the system on executive, legislative and judicial fronts. Many of those who advocated more government aid for educating handicapped children saw themselves as part of the mainstream of politics, in the same manner as did the major civil rights groups, and set about to organize themselves in advancing the cause of the handicapped.

Education of the Handicapped in the Early Years

Who went to school? Everyone? Probably not, for the handicapped — the deaf, the blind and the orthopedically impaired, the mentally ill and emotionally disturbed, and the retarded — were not considered "teachable" in the traditional sense and were thus left out of the educational system, dependent on their families for their emotional and financial support and for what "learning" they could absorb in day-to-day living. If private charitable, religious and philanthropic organizations did their part to alleviate the plight of the handicapped, fine. If government took any responsibility, it was to provide institutions to care for them, and no effort was made to bring the handicapped into the mainstream of society. The handicapped were discriminated against and could never enjoy the fruits of maturity or citizenship. They were shunted aside and remained so until the middle of the twentieth century when, at long last, under the pressures generated at first by a few and then by many, government began to take a closer look and ask: what can be done, and by whom?

Special education programs began in some states as early as the 1820's with the establishment of state schools for the deaf and the blind, and later for the mentally retarded. In the early 1900's, these efforts expanded in the more progressive states to include, as in Massachusetts, requirements that special classes must be provided for the mentally retarded by local school boards who could identify 10 or more such children. This movement was slow but, until the middle 1950's, progress was constant on the state level.

The federal government did not accept much responsibility for educating the handicapped until recently. Early programs in this area were financially limited and aimed at solving individual problems of specific disability groups. The earliest legislation provided funds to establish schools for the blind and deaf and to construct facilities for the insane. In 1879, Congress authorized the establishment of the American Printing House for the Blind. Traditionally, federal legislation was the result of a specific need on the part of a special disability group or because of one-time events or circumstances; i.e., rehabilitation services for disabled war veterans.[2]

In the 1960's, however, the cause of the handicapped was boosted to national attention partly because President John F. Kennedy publicly acknowledged having a retarded sister. Kennedy's personal interest in this area led to his appointment in 1961 of the *President's Panel on Mental Retardation* which was charged with developing recommendations to combat retardation on a national scale. Several of the recommendations of the task force were later enacted into law by Congress and augmented the grievously underfunded research and training activities already authorized.[3] The handicapped, however, were still excluded from full participation in society. Handicapped children in particular were not viewed as entitled to receive educational services on a par with the non-handicapped in the public schools.

A basic assumption underlined the perception society had

[2] Martin L. Lavor, "Federal Legislation for Exceptional Persons; A History," Fred J. Weintraub *et al.*, ed., *Public Policy and the Education of Exceptional Children*, Reston, Va., 1976, 99.

[3] *Ibid.*, 100.

of the handicapped — that they had problems in society because of their handicap, not because they lacked the education necessary for them to compete in the society and enjoy a full life. Programs were aimed at correcting the handicap, altering the individual so that he or she could adapt. They were not aimed at upgrading the life of the handicapped, despite their handicap, or at changing the attitudes of the non-handicapped society towards the handicapped. The handicapped were interested in correcting the system so that the system could adapt to them, so that each handicapped individual would be given access to the society and have an opportunity to participate equitably according to his or her potential.[4] In short, there was no concerted effort on the part of either society or government to bring handicapped people into the mainstream of the society. Handicapped children, in particular, were not in the mainstream of the public educational system.

NARC AND CEC: MAJOR ADVOCATES FOR THE HANDICAPPED

An advocacy movement begins when those being discriminated against become fed up and politically band together for the purpose of adjusting the system to accommodate them. In the case of the handicapped, groups of parents whose children had similar disabilities formed around the country to provide comfort for each other and to work politically for change.

As early as 1933, parents in an Ohio county came together to express their "indignation" that their children had been excluded from the public school. While this meeting had

[4] Rita A. Varela, "Self Advocacy and Changing Attitudes in *Public Awareness Viewpoints*," in Gary Richman and Pascal Trohanis, eds., *Developmental Disabilities Technical Assistance System*, June, 1978, 30-31.

no immediate impact on the system, it represents the type of new awareness that was developing across the country. While such activities were not uncommon in the 1930's and forties, these fledgling organizations did not constitute a national movement as such. They maintained no communication with each other and limited their aims to making handicapped children's lives as pleasant as possible. Parent organizations, however, served several purposes. They served as an outlet for the frustrations of their members; they provided support for actions to obtain improved services for their children; and they provided the foundation for a more widely based program of action.[5]

During the 1950's a new awareness of the problems of the handicapped developed. There was an obvious need to pay attention to these problems at the State and local level, not to mention the national.[6] This new awareness became the catalyst for further oganization of parent groups at the national level and the expansion of the handicapped constituency.

Two national groups stand out as early examples of advocates for the handicapped: The National Association for Retarded Citizens (NARC) and the Council for Exceptional Children (CEC). NARC is primarily an organization of people, usually parents and family, with a personal interest in retarded persons. Its mission is to provide information, monitor the quality of service given to the retarded and serve as an advocate for the rights and interests of retarded children and adults. NARC was organized in September, 1950 and was the gathering together of several State organizations of parents and families of retarded individuals. Delegates from 23 organizations in 13 States were present at the NARC

[5] *MR 76, Mental Retardation: Past and Present*, Government Printing Office, Washington, D.C. January 1977, 37.

[6] Leopold Lippman and I. Ignacy Goldberg, *Right to Education: Anatomy of the Pennsylvania Case and its Implications for Exceptional Children*, New York: Teachers College Press, 1973).

organizational meeting in 1950. By 1960 there were 681 State and local chapters and 62,000 members. In 1975, NARC boasted a membership of 218,000 and 1,700 State and local chapters. (NARC is an example of thousands of interest groups whose organizational structure parallels the federal nature of the American political system. To be nationally effective, the group must be able to pressure not only the federal but also state and local government. When organizations in several states link up and enter the national political arena, it is an indication of their political maturity and growing strength. Thus they can now bring the Congress into the scope fo their operations.)

The Council for Exceptional Children (CEC) represents mainly special education professionals whose concern is for all children with special needs and whose purpose is to improve educational services to "exceptional" children and youth, whether gifted or handicapped. CEC was founded in 1922 by some faculty and students at Teachers College, Columbia University, in New York. While its early growth was slow, membership in the council has grown from 6,000 members in 1950 to approximately 70,000. CEC is heavily involved in advocating the rights of handicapped children and has been in the forefront of the movement to obtain these rights on the federal and state levels. Most of the several million handicapped children in the nation are surrounded by family, teachers, and friends who are concerned about obtaining the optimum benefits from society for them. NARC and CEC are two of the many organizations that represent these interests in government and played a major role in bringing PL 94-142 to fruition.

EXPANDING THE SCOPE OF CONFLICT

When any group wishes to assert its will in the political decision-making process, it must decide whether to bring into the fray other like-minded groups to support its position, thus broadening the scope of conflict, or keep the conflict as confined as possible in order to retain control of the process. The former method is called "expanding the scope of conflict" and the latter "narrowing the scope of conflict."[7] There is danger, however, in expanding the conflict in that opposing interest groups might find it necessary to organize strong opposition because of the gathering strength of the expanding number of groups seeking something. It would be thus more difficult, under such a set of conditions, for the original group to win the day. On the other hand, narrowing the scope of conflict limits the political activity of the primary group because of the necessity to keep the opposition unaware (and thus off balance) as much as possible. If it appears to the opposition that there is little danger of their opponents obtaining anything important, it might simply lay low, believing the issue is not worth contending. Usually, interest groups expand the conflict when they seek something new, or something added to what they already have, as they attempt to extract from a legislative body both programs and funds to support their cause. They hope, then, that their case is so powerful, and they are so articulate in presenting it, that they can overcome any opposition that might emerge from the expansion of the conflict. When interest groups attempt to keep something from happening, that is when they seek to pinch off legislative action at some critical point in the process, they usually keep their activity confined to that point of access. Therefore they try to narrow the scope of conflict. Expanding is essentially rooted in the seeking of positive legislation — gaining something — while narrowing is tied to negating legislation — to keep something from happening.

Interest groups for handicapped children fell into the

---

[7] See the seminal work of E. E. Schattschneider, *The Semi-Sovereign People*, (New York: Holt-Rinehart-Winston, 1960).

"positive" category, since they found it necessary to expand the scope of conflict. The important element in their "expansion," however, was that no opposing interest groups at first came to the front to battle against them. There were two reasons for this. The requests of the handicapped did not seem excessive and, more important, one could hardly combat handicapped children as being unworthy of legislative consideration. The early interest groups for handicapped children, therefore, were able to build their case by bringing together other like-minded groups (particularly in the education community). Generally speaking, the scenario could go something like this. Let us say that the Council for Exceptional Children wants to elicit support from the Congress in an area with which Congress has not been very much concerned. It brings onto its side another like-minded group, such as the National Association for Retarded Citizens. To strengthen their combined position before the various legislative committees, these two groups might then reach out and gather under a wider umbrella a number of other groups, each concerned with a particular aspect of the problems of the handicapped — the deaf, the blind, the physically impaired, etc. The term *handicapped* covers a wide range of specific handicaps. Were these interest groups to take a path which related their handicaps to "health" as opposed to "education," their approach to solving the problems of handicapped children would be different. Education, which falls under a different jurisdiction in the Congressional committee system than health, is a better context for changing the system. Health-related services to handicapped children imply some sort of compensation or adaptation of the handicapped to the system. On the other hand, health-related services are a necessary prerequisite, and indeed requirement, for a total educational program for handicapped children. Thus two purposes could be served by going the education route in the Congress: obtaining new programs and funds from the federal and state governments to facilitate *both* education *and* health needs. Were the health context the first principle, the need for education programs might not necessarily be a properly drawn conclusion. To begin with, then, education became the vehicle for the interest groups to ride in their attempts to bring about a better life for handicapped children. That, in brief, was the general direction the interest groups took.

EARLY FEDERAL PROGRAMS IN SPECIAL EDUCATION

Between 1965, when Congress passed the Elementary and Secondary Education Act (PL 89-10), and 1975, when the Education for All Handicapped Children Act (PL 94-142) was enacted, organized handicapped groups slowly grew in importance and magnitude. At first, they were disunited, each working on the state and federal levels for additional programs and funds benefitting its own constituency. The federal government, despite the concerns earlier voiced by President John F. Kennedy, did little for the handicapped. Relatively few Senators and Representatives and their staffs could point to educating handicapped children as high on their list of priorities.

As part of President Lyndon B. Johnson's war on poverty and in keeping with the context of the times, Congress enacted the Elementary and Secondary Education Act in 1965. PL 89-10 was a congressional response as well to the interest groups which had been petitioning both federal and state government for more funds for compensatory education for the economically underprivileged. There was also a close tie-in to the civil rights movement. Interest groups advocating aid for handicapped children hoped eventually to link themselves with the then current sense of urgency for the underprivileged. Before we see how that linkage came about in 1966, an explanation of the Elementary and Secondary Education Act of 1965 is in order.

Title I provided the states with federal funds to cover the "excess costs" to meet the needs of educationally deprived children in school districts with high concentrations of low-income families. Such districts could not afford the high cost of education because their tax bases, rooted in property taxes at the local level, were very low. The handicapped, to be sure, could receive services under Title I, but Title I was directed at providing compensatory education to children who were educationally disadvantaged because of low income, not handicaps. Title II of the ESEA of 1965 dealt with funds for library resources, textbooks, and other instructional material (essentially aid to the school districts), while Title III was aimed at enriching programs for guidance and counseling, remedial instruction, school health, recreation, psychological and social work, and special educational projects. Treatment for handicapped children under Title III was not considered an essential aspect of ESEA. Title IV and V earmarked funds for educational research, training, and strengthening state departments of education. There was, then, no clearcut relationship between ESEA and programs for handicapped children in 1965, and the Elementary and Secondary Education Act was authorized for only one year. It had to be renewed, after oversight procedures by the Congress, which were to begin in 1966.

Interest Groups Make Their Move: Amending ESEA, Title VI, 1966

In 1965 the number of children and youth in the United States requiring some form of special education because of physical and/or mental handicap was estimated to be somewhere between five and seven million. Only about 25 per cent of them were actually enrolled in public or private school, taught by about 60,000 special education teachers in the nation's public schools and about 11,000 in private schools. To educate and service all the handicapped of school age would require 300,000 teachers.[8] The costs of public school education were borne primarily by state and local government. The federal government assisted the states in educating the nation's handicapped children and youth to a very minor degree, attaching some appropriations to bills which did not deal directly with handicapped children. In fiscal 1964, for example, only one million dollars of federal funds were expended for research and demonstration projects through federal/state grant-in-aid programs, to which another million was added for fiscal 1965. These projects were supposedly designed to translate research findings into practical application for the teaching of handicapped children. Spreading this rather paltry sum among the various research projects carried out by universities and private institutions for special education resulted in far too little help for the many in need. The handicapped, at that time, were legislatively defined as the deaf, emotionally disturbed, mentally retarded, visually handicapped, crippled and other health-impaired children. In 1965 and 1966, only 68 projects were funded throughout the country. Given the nature of the problem, federal funds created hardly a ripple; clearly the cost of educating a handicapped child was far greater than that needed to educate one without special problems.

Training and supplying teachers for the handicapped were not getting very far in the middle 1960's. How fared handicapped children? They and their families were hardly an

---

[8] *Hearings on the Education of Handicapped Children*, Senate Subcommittee on Health of the Senate Committee on Labor and Public Welfare, 89th Cong., 1st Sess., May 17, 1965, 13-45. And, *Hearings on Education and Training of the Handicapped*, House Ad Hoc Subcommittee on the Handicapped, House Committee on Education and Labor, 89th Cong., 2nd Sess., 1966, 144-146.

organized interest group. In fact, different handicaps had different groups advocating programs and funds. They rarely coordinated their efforts. The handicapped labored under a major problem. State and local agencies generally wanted to set the handicapped far aside — to sweep them under the rug, so to speak — for to "service" the handicapped with special educational programs was far too costly given limited state and local funds. State and local education agencies complained that they could not afford to upgrade educational opportunities in their regular elementary and secondary schools, let alone for the handicapped.

In 1965, President Johnson established a Task Force on the Reorganization of the Office of Education in the Department of Health, Education and Welfare. In June of that year the Task Force issued a report which recommended in principle the decentralization of the Office of Education. The interest groups with offices in Washington and which represented the education community took strong exception to this move, fearing that their effectiveness pressuring the federal government would be lessened by a diffusion of executive responsibility. Those interested in handicapped children were particularly concerned that decentralization would make it even more difficult for them to focus attention on the needs of the handicapped. The Council for Exceptional Children seized the opportunity to begin lobbying for an explicit bureau within the Office of Education to administer programs for the handicapped and thus give the handicapped a federal office on which to focus and concentrate their attention. The vehicle for this lobbying effort in the Senate was a bill, S. 3046, submitted to the Senate in March, 1966 by Senator Wayne Morse (Democrat of Oregon), the chairman of the Senate Subcommittee on Education of the Senate Committee on Labor and Public Welfare. Senator Morse, a staunch advocate of more federal aid for handicapped children, decided that the educational committee of the Senate, his Subcommittee, would take jurisdiction, thus eliminating the Subcommittee on Health from the issue. This was a move of course that was urged and applauded by the handicapped, for it fit into their approach to have the handicapped go through the educational jurisdiction rather than the health jurisdiction of the committee system. A strong Senator on the Republican side of Morse's Subcommittee, who also was particularly interested in the plight of the handicapped, was Senator Winston Prouty of Vermont. Senator Prouty deeply believed that there should be a specific office in the government that would be a focal point for the problems of handicapped children.

S. 3046, basically, was the re-authorization of ESEA. Primary attention of Morse's Subcommittee focused on that issue in the Subcommittee's hearings in 1966. There was no special subcommittee on the handicapped in the Senate, and Morse's Subcommittee on Education had been recently assigned jurisdiction over handicapped legislation at Morse's behest. In six days of testimony on S. 3046 in April, 1966, barely a couple of hours were devoted to the needs of handicapped children. The United States Commissioner of Education, who headed up OE, told Senator Prouty that there was not a great deal of movement on the matter by the federal government.[9] William Geer, the executive Secretary of the Council for Exceptional Children, urged the Senate to write into law some sort of mandated federal aid, pointing out that state programs to aid handicapped children were very uneven. Those states which operated special education programs were still serving only a fraction of their total handicapped population. Geer noted that: first, the ESEA was not viewed by the states as a federal program to benefit children with disabilities; second, many states felt their own programs for serving the handicapped were adequate; third, much confusion

---

[9] *Hearings, ESEA of 1966*, Subcommittee on Education, Senate Committee on Labor and Public Welfare, 89th Cong., 2nd Sess., April, 1966, 341-342.

reigned as to whether or not the handicapped children could be counted for Title I only if they also qualified as living in low-income families; and fourth, the states were not adequately staffed to promote state assistance and guidelines to local school districts in this area. The CEC supported both increased federal assistance to the states and more federal influence on the states.[10]

Of the 2,600 pages of Senate hearings, only a few dealt with the problems of educating handicapped children. The record addressed primarily the issues surrounding extension of ESEA. But within the confines of the Subcommittee's offices, the staff of the Subcommittee was very much aware of the need for legislation. Both Senators Morse and Prouty were bent on doing something.

The public record in 1966, on behalf of the handicapped, was made in the House of Representatives where an *Ad Hoc* Subcommittee on the Handicapped of the House Committee on Education and Labor looked more carefully and exactly on the problem.

THE CAREY HOUSE SUBCOMMITTEE ON THE HANDICAPPED

The House companion bill to S. 3046, extending and reauthorizing the ESEA, was H.R. 13161 which was before the House Committee on Education and Labor. An *Ad Hoc* Subcommittee on the Handicapped, under the chairmanship of Congressman Hugh L. Carey (Democrat of New York) had been created by the full Committee. While the former could devote its time to H.R. 13161, which dealt only with extending ESEA, Carey's Subcommittee could go into far more detail about handicapped children and their problems. In June, 1966, Carey's Subcommittee held eight oversight

[10]*Ibid.*, 1786-1788.

hearings to investigate the adequacy of federal and other resources for educating and training the handicapped. Interest groups for the handicapped thus had more opportunity to pack the record with evidence of the need for federal assistance to educate and serve the handicapped.

The Staff Director of Carey's Subcommittee was Dr. Edwin W. Martin, Jr., who was deeply concerned about the needs of handicapped children. (In 1980 he would become Assistant Secretary of Education.) The four Democrats and two Republicans on the Subcommittee leaned heavily towards the "liberal" point of view and generally the Subcommittee was committed to a greater role for the federal government in educating handicapped children. Eleven interest groups for the handicapped had their representatives, or lobbyists, testify at the Carey hearings in June, 1966.

When conducting oversight hearings, a committee calls on a senior official to give the Administration's views and to testify about the effectiveness of the agency's implementation of federal law. At that time the Office of Education in HEW had within it a small group to handle matters relating to the disadvantaged and handicapped. But the Carey subcommittee called on Commissioner of Education Harold Howe II to testify about the efficacy of ESEA and benefits to the handicapped under the 1965 law. Howe testified that Titles I through V of the ESEA of 1965 did have "some component of service to the handicapped." He tried to make a strong case out of a weak one by arguing that Titles I through V were being effectively utilized for the handicapped. But Carey forcefully pointed out that the nation urgently needed a national policy for educating the handicapped.[11] The Bureau of Elementary and Secondary Education in OE could show that only 68 of the 484 project

---

[11] *Hearings on Education and Training of the Handicapped, Ad Hoc* Subcommittee on the Handicapped, House Committee on Education and Labor, 89th Cong., 2nd Sess., Part 1, 1966, p. 40.

applications from the states under PL 89-10 (ESEA of 1965) were tied to programs for the handicapped and of these 68 only a handful could rightly be classified as *specifically* for the handicapped. Only 5 per cent (135 out of 2,846) of the additional teaching personnel hired under ESEA could be categorized as special teachers for the handicapped. Clearly the states were not anxious to direct federal funds for general education under ESEA to aid for the handicapped. As Arthur L. Harris of the Bureau of Elementary and Secondary Education pointed out to the Carey subcommittee, ". . .it [was] evident that many local education agencies, for whatever reasons, [did] not always choose to put substantial amounts of money into projects expressly designed for handicapped children." State and local education agencies simply made little effort to involve the handicapped, and Harris stated that local education agencies had to make a very special effort even to identify the handicapped in their school districts. The primary initiative for programs had to come from the local school districts, school officials, and special education leaders in the community. Understandably, from the point of view of local school districts, cost was a vital factor. The average per pupil expenditure at that time for education services ranged from $300 to $500. The cost for educating a handicapped child, however, was somewhere between $1,000 and $2,000 annually. Diverting money from the general education program serving most of the community to meet the needs of a few was not looked upon with favor. As a result, most local communities had "patchwork or hit-and-miss programs for aid to the handicapped." Harris then told the Carey subcommittee that this reluctance on the part of local educational agencies could be overcome by earmarking a percentage of the appropriation to be "available for the education of handicapped children, to be available for that purpose and no other purposes."[12] (This method of funding

12 *Ibid.*, 58-73.

has come to be termed "set asides" because programs paid for in this manner are always and must be fully funded as the first allocation.)

Given the needs of the millions of handicapped children in the nation and the reluctance of the states and local educational agencies to satisfy those needs, the federal involvement would have to increase as would the federal incentive programs for the states in some sort of grant-in-aid method. Otherwise there would be no solution.

Before groups advocating increased programs and funds for handicapped children presented their views in testimony before the Carey Subcommittee, Donald N. Bigelow, the Acting Director of the Division of Educational Personnel Training of the Bureau of Elementary and Secondary Education in OE, expressed what would years later become a dominant theme. Among other things, there should be established, he said, "a positive attitude toward integrating the education of the handicapped in the *total school program* (italics added) while still continuing to provide for special needs." The time had to come to realize that "the education of the handicapped is an important, relatively small, but integral part of elementary and secondary education." A major concern was just how to "mainstream" the education of handicapped children into the total school program at the elementary and secondary school level.[13] The issue of "mainstreaming" would later become a principal source of friction between parents of handicapped children and local educational agencies.

Interest Groups and the Carey Subcommittee, 1966

Interest groups for handicapped children testifying in June were there to place their viewpoints about the needs of handi-

[13] *Ibid.*, 120-121.

capped children on the public record. Their main themes were: first, federal funds in sufficient amounts were needed by the states for compensatory education for handicapped children; second, a central, important administrative entity within the executive branch was necessary to advance the cause of handicapped children; and third, a free public education that was *appropriate for each child's disability* in one way or another, had to be mandated upon the states. Handicapped children needed counseling, guidance, transportation, vocational services, training, job placement and so on. The entire handicapped program was piecemeal and inadequate with fifty different definitions of handicapped because each of the fifty states adhered to its own version and practices.[14] The following interest groups presented their views in testimony: American Psychological Association, National Association of Mental Health, Alexander Graham Bell Association for the Deaf, Institute for Research on Exceptional Children, Council on Education of the Deaf, Association for Children with Learning Disabilities, American Foundation for the Blind, American Speech and Hearing Association, National Association for Retarded Citizens (NARC), National Rehabilitation Association, and the Council for Exceptional Children (CEC).

Each group represented a particular handicapped constituency, ranging from the deaf to the blind, the mentally retarded to the emotionally disturbed. Not all were in exact accord with what should be done. The CEC, for example, was somewhat fearful that the gifted child, who was just as "handicapped" in a classroom with "regular" students as the physically and mentally handicapped, might be overlooked in the quest for federal financial assistance. The Council recommended that a Bureau for Exceptional Children be established to administer programs for the gifted as well. The majority of the statements made by the various

[14] *Ibid.*, 551.

interest groups stressed the lack of space for teaching handicapped children in the public schools, the inadequacy of state
and local funds to educate the millions of handicapped
children, and the absence of a coordinated national policy.

At this time, the interest groups knew that the attain-
ment of one of their major goals was in the offing. Carey's
Subcommittee staff, working closely with that of the CEC,
was committed to the creation of an executive bureau for
the education of handicapped children. The staff of the
Senate Subcommittee on Education was also sympathetic
with this aim. The hearing record contains some impressive
documentation of the need for a special entity within the
Office of Education.

Hugh Carey, New York's Congressman who would later
be elected Governor, was encouraged by Congressman John
Fogarty (Democrat of Rhode Island) who also had a personal
commitment to aid the handicapped. After the June hearings,
Carey introduced H.R. 16847 in the House. The bill was
drafted by Edwin Martin, Carey's staffer, and was intended
to be used as a vehicle to amend S. 3046. The staff of the
Senate Subcommittee on Education joined Martin in an
effort to upgrade representation of the handicapped in the
executive branch. Carey wanted to be sure that there were
similar provisions for both the Senate and House versions of
ESEA when the Senate and House went into conference to
iron out differences between S. 3046 and H.R. 13161. Since
the Senate had already finished the hearings on S. 3046 and
the House was not directly dealing with handicapped problems in H.R. 13161, Carey's bill, H.R. 16847, could be the
vehicle for publicizing in hearings before Carey's Subcommittee what was to come out of conference later in the year.

Carey's H.R. 16847 authorized a formula grant program to
assist state and local educational agencies in establishing programs for handicapped children. In order to qualify for federal funds, however, the states taking part in the program,
had to provide effective procedures to bridge the gap

between research on the teaching of the handicapped and the general application of the results of that research to the teaching itself. Carey's bill would provide financial support for acquisition and development of instructional material; the development of centers to teach the handicapped; the development of models for regular programs of special education; and, the means for recruiting personnel into the field of teaching the handicapped. A major feature of Carey's bill was to establish a Bureau of Education for the Handicapped to be located within the Office of Education of HEW and a National Advisory Committee on Education and Training of the Handicapped. BEH, as it became known, would help "bring special education into the mainstream of education," and the National Advisory Committee would help establish "better communication between the field of special education and the Federal Government."[15]

During hearings in August on H.R. 16847, ten witnesses testified in support of the proposal. The Office of Education, however, was not pleased with Carey's proposals. J. Graham Sullivan, Deputy Commissioner of Education, appeared before the Subcommittee to urge a delay in further legislation for the handicapped on the grounds that the ESEA should be given a chance to work. In addition, he said, OE did not want Congress to legislate "internal administrative structures."[16] Taking exception to Sullivan's position, Carey reminded the Deputy Commissioner that the Subcommittee had elicited from Arthur Harris of the Bureau of Elementary and Secondary Education of OE the admission that "there was no national policy on the handicapped. None was being evolved and nothing was being undertaken."[17] The Chairman of the Subcommittee went on to point out that President Johnson had also taken note of this problem and established his own task force to study it. In fact, 27 in-

[15] *Ibid.*, p. 763.
[16] *Ibid.*, 709.
[17] *Ibid.*, 713.

terest groups for the handicapped had been invited to participate in the work of the task force.[18] Carey argued that the Office of Education was engaging in delay and obfuscation, and he was insistent that his bill, if incorporated into S. 3046 and H.R. 13161, would move the executive branch and the states faster along the road of providing a better and more fulfilling education for the nation's handicapped children.

Creation of Title VI in PL 89–750, 1966

The staffs of the Senate Subcommittee on Education and Carey's Subcommittee on the Handicapped struck a deal, inserting the provisions of H.R. 16847 into the ESEA amendments as a new Title VI of the ESEA within the scope of S. 3046. On October 3, 1966, the Senate Subcommittee on Labor and Public Welfare reported out its version of S. 3046, containing the new Title VI. Three days later the Senate passed the bill easily. Since the House had already passed its ESEA reauthorization in the form of H.R. 13161 without any reference to the same handicapped provisions and as there were differences between H.R. 13161 and S. 3046 anyway, the Senate and House now had to go into a joint conference committee to come to a mutual agreement. A joint conference committee is not authorized by either house to insert brand new material in the final bill, but because the Senate's bill, S. 3046, had had the provisions of H.R. 16847 added to it before passage by the Senate, it was now legitimate to include it in the final bill presented to both houses. House conferees were amenable to the inclusion of Title VI, and after compromising on other aspects of the ESEA, the joint conference committee reported the conference bill to the Senate and the House. Emerging from the joint conference committee, then, was a bill which now contained a new

[18] *Ibid.*, 809.

Title VI and which sailed through both houses of Congress, as S. 3046. President Johnson signed the bill into law and it became Public Law 89-750.[19]

The interest groups for the handicapped had managed to have attached to an Act of Congress a new program which had not been challenged on the floor of either house.[20] The Senate had not considered Title VI in any great detail, since it had been added to S. 3046 by the Subcommittee on Education and approved without any problem at all by the Senate Committee on Labor and Public Welfare. The House had never debated the issue, although the Carey Subcommittee on the Handicapped had aired all the pros (and few of the cons) of Title VI through open hearings. The result was exactly what proponents for more educational services for handicapped children wanted at the moment, a foothold in education. From this they could continue to build.

In summary, Title VI authorized about $50 million for fiscal 1967 and $150 million for fiscal 1968 to assist the states in "the initiation, expansion, and improvement of programs and projects . . . for the education of handicapped children at the preschool, elementary and secondary education levels." (It must be remembered that "authorizations" are not "appropriations" which must be made by the Congress in separate legislation for the fiscal years.) Handicapped children were now defined as the "mentally retarded, hard of hearing, deaf, speech impaired, visually handicapped, seriously emotionally disturbed, crippled or other health impaired children." This was a broad definition. No mention was made in Title VI of placing or "mainstreaming" handicapped children directly into the public school classroom,

[19] PL 89-750, U.S. Statutes at Large, 89th Cong., 2nd Sess., 1966, Vol. 80, Part I, 1204-1208.

[20] Senate Report No. 1674, *Amendments of the ESEA of 1966,* October 3, 1966. House Report No. 2309, *Elementary and Secondary Education Amendments of 1966,* Conference Report, October 18, 1966.

nor did Title VI recognize that access to a free, appropriate public education was a "right." If a state desired to take part in a program to facilitate the teaching of handicapped children with federal funds supplied for excess costs of such education, it would have to conform "through its State educational agency" to the detailed guide-lines established by the U.S. Commissioner of Education. But there was nothing as of 1966 that *required* a state to take part in the program.

The real importance of Title VI was the establishment in OE of the Bureau of Education for the Handicapped, which was to be the principal agency in the Office of Education for administering and carrying out the programs and projects for the education and training of handicapped children. Under pressure of House leadership, the Johnson Administration chose Dr. Edwin Martin, Carey's staffer on the Subcommittee for the Handicapped to head up the new bureau. The House advocates for education for handicapped children would now have "their man" in OE. They had pressed the Administration to appoint Martin to head off the selection of one of the Senate staffers or one of the insiders in HEW.

For the first time, handicapped children and their families had a federal office to call their own. As Congress conducted future oversight hearings on education for the handicapped, its appropriate committees could zero in on specific federal agency officials who had been charged by law to carry out the intent of the Congress. A new relationship could also develop between the executive branch through the BEH and the National Advisory Committee which had also been established by Title VI to act as a consultant body to the BEH and Congress. Also important, however, was the precedent which was set by the establishment of BEH. The Congress had legislated the internal organization of the Office of Education. The fact that this was done indicated not only the growing influence of the handicapped in national affairs, but also the political power of the Congress as it was beginning to assert itself over the executive branch.

The Education of the Handicapped Act, PL 91-230, April, 1970.

Despite Congressional commitment to the authorization of several millions for handicapped programs, when the Congress finished with the President's Budget, funds actually appropriated for educating the handicapped under Title VI were only about 25 per cent of the original authorizations. The lag between funds authorized and actually appropriated (appropriations must be within the context of the overall Presidential Budget) caused the leading interest groups for handicapped children to redouble their efforts to pressure the executive branch to seek more funds from the Congress. The Nixon Administration was now in power and was not very committed to increasing expenditures for this area of federal spending, although the Bureau of Education for the Handicapped and the National Advisory Committee of course were so committed. Without some sort of enforced cooperation between the executive and the Congress, handicapped groups would not be able to fulfill their expectations very easily. One way to obtain more money was to increase the authorizations, and even though the percentage of the funds actually appropriated might be the same as before, at least the real funds would then have been increased. Leading groups for the handicapped drew closer to their counterparts in the committee system in Congress in 1968 and 1969 to further this aim. They had their allies in the BEH and the National Advisory Committee, but the former was not strong enough within the Office of Education, not adequately staffed, and had not yet sunk its roots deeply enough in the education community. The goal of the Nixon administration was to restrain spending, not expand it, and thus the administration was an obstacle to the aims of the BEH and the interest groups.

The National Advisory Committee was chaired by Dr. Samuel A. Kirk of the Department of Special Education at the University of Arizona and was still "feeling its way" through the complexities of the relationships among the Congress, interest groups and the executive branch. Nevertheless, the National Advisory Committee, recipient of pressure and lobbying from the handicapped interest groups and in sympathy with the progress they wished to make, argued strongly for increasing the stature of the handicapped community in the political process. The Committee argued principally for: (1) full funding of Title VI; (2) increasing the number of special education teachers; (3) correcting misclassifications of disadvantaged children as handicapped; (4) increasing the number of BEH personnel; and (5) encouraging the states to coordinate each of their individual federal educational programs for handicapped children through a single state advisory committee.

Despite the limitations imposed on the BEH by the shortage of funds, it had organized seven regional conferences for 1,000 special educators in 1968 to help establish a partnership between the states and the federal government. The BEH had also begun work on establishing management information systems to the states, organizing and funding two research and development centers, and starting several demonstration projects and programs. BEH was also responsible for handling state allocations under Title VI and for "approving" state plans for educating handicapped children as being in conformity with federal regulations.

The National Advisory Committee on Handicapped Children became the "in-house" arm for handicapped children. It officially took note that authorized programs for handicapped children had to be nourished or they would "lapse into a state of atrophy."[21] The Committee continually stressed that 60 per cent of the then estimated 6 million handicapped children in the United States received *no*

---

[21] *Second Annual Report* of the National Advisory Committee on Handicapped Children, 1969, 7.

special educational services and that production of new professionals to teach them was not at all high enough to serve them properly.[22]

Oversight hearings to extend and expand elementary and secondary educational programs for handicapped children were held in 1969.[23] The two-and-a-half-year-old Title VI had indeed had some positive impact on the issues. It had

> helped state and local agencies to raise the quality of assistance they had been offering to school–aged handicapped children . . . prompted a greater awareness of the special needs of handicapped children among school administrators, both regular and special education teachers and the general public . . . supported administrative personnel at all levels. . .and sparked better cooperation and communication among the many agencies dealing with the handicapped.[24]

Dr. Samuel Kirk (the Chairman of the National Advisory Committee, who also represented the Association of Children with Learning Disabilities) urged Congress to add another category to the definition of handicapped children. One to three per cent of the nation's school population had "special" or "specific" learning disabilities related to listening, thinking, talking, reading, writing, spelling or calculating arithmetic because of psychological defects that inhibit the learning process, unrelated to mental retardation or emotional disturbances.[25] Except for this innovative request, however, most of the testimony at the hearings reiterated the

[22] *Ibid.*, 31.

[23] *Hearings on H.R. 514*, House Committee on Education and Labor, parts 1 and 2, 89th Cong., 1st sess., 1969 and *Hearings on S. 2218* and H.R. 514, Senate Subcommittee on Education, parts 1 and 2, 89th Cong., 1st sess., 1969.

[24] *Ibid.*, senate hearings, 1145.

[25] *Ibid.*, 907-908.

need for a longer period of time for the authorization of the extension of Title VI.

Congress responded by passing legislation replacing Title VI with the Education of The Handicapped Act. The definition of a handicapped child was not changed from that written into the law as Title VI in 1966. But PL 91-230 established the authority for the Office of Education to make grants to institutions of higher education, state and local education agencies, and other public and private educational and research agencies to carry out a program of research and training in the field of "specific learning disabilities," thus adding a new category for federal involvement in education.

Children with specific learning disabilities were defined as children with a "disorder in one or more of the basic psychological processes involved in or in using language, spoken or written . . ." These disorders were rooted in "such conditions as perceptual handicaps, brain injury, minimal brain dysfunction, dyslexia, and developmental aphasia." To pay for the program on specific learning disabilities, the Congress authorized $94 million spread out in the next four fiscal years.

For assistance to the states for education of handicapped children, the Congress also upped the authorizations from the previous law ($630 million to June 30, 1973). The sum of $153.5 million was authorized for centers and services to meet the special needs of the handicapped (including early education of pre-school age handicapped children). For research and demonstration projects in education of handicapped children, the authorization was $107.5 million; for training personnel for educating handicapped children, $260 million; for establishing a system of educational media and materials for the handicapped, $47.5 million. The authority for these programs would terminate on June 30, 1973, at which time they would have to be extended or dropped. And, of course, allocation of funds through the appropriations process required further legislation for each fiscal year.

Court Litigation: The P.A.R.C. and Mills Decisions

Groups representing handicapped children were not directing their efforts and energies only towards passage of favorable
legislation. If they could get the courts to rule that education
for handicapped children was a constitutional requirement,
their position before Congress, state and local government
would be much strengthened. Laws in all states mandated that
children had to attend school for a certain number of years
or up to a specific age. If handicapped children were being
shunted aside by the school systems simply because educating them was an inconvenience to the educational agencies,
then the handicapped might be able to make a civil rights
case out of their exclusion from the mainstream of public
education. The courts thus became another vehicle for establishing government's responsibilities to handicapped children.
Most of the cases filed in state and federal courts focused on
three issues: 1) the right of handicapped children to an
appropriate publicly supported education; 2) the right to
treatment including education for children in institutions;
and 3) the use of improper classification and placement to
discriminate against children with handicaps in the provision
of education.[26]

In January, 1971, the Pennsylvania Association for Retarded Children (P.A.R.C.) brought suit in the Federal District Court for the Eastern Pennsylvania District against the
state of Pennsylvania for its failure to provide *all* retarded
children access to a free, public education. P.A.R.C.'s class
action suit on behalf of 14 mentally retarded children of
school age and "all others similarly situated" in the state was
specifically brought against the state's Secretaries of Education and Public Welfare, Board of Education, and thirteen
named school districts. In essence, P.A.R.C. argued that
mentally retarded children were not receiving their full right

[26] Alan Abeson, "Litigation," Weintraub et al., *op cit.*, 240.

to an education because the state was delaying or ignoring its constitutional obligations to provide a publicly supported education to the retarded, the same education that state law and the Equal Protection of the Laws Clause of the 14th Amendment of the United States Constitution required. As long as publicly supported education was mandated by the State of Pennsylvania, said P.A.R.C., it was obligated to give that same education to all children, regardless of physical or mental handicaps. Even though Pennsylvania took part in the federal-state program for educating the handicapped, not all its handicapped children were being educated. Pennsylvania was hiding behind the cloak of its own laws and practices to exclude, postpone, or deny free access to public education opportunities to school age mentally retarded children. P.A.R.C. now asked the Federal District Court to make such an education mandatory. Nine months later, a three–judge panel unanimously ruled that all retarded children in the State between six and twenty-one years of age had to be provided, as a constitutional right and state statutory requirement, a publicly supported education. Furthermore, said the Court, it was most desirable to educate these children in a program most like that provided for non-handicapped children.

Pennsylvania then entered into a consent agreement, thus closing off appeals and thereby setting the stage for the decision to become precedent for suits in other states. The P.A.R.C. decision can be read alongside the 1972 Mills decision.

A class action suit, similar to that in P.A.R.C., was brought in 1971 in the Federal District Court for the District of Columbia by the parents and guardians of seven District of Columbia children who were afflicted with handicaps of slight brain damage, hyperactive behavior, epilepsy and mental retardation, and orthopedic impairment against the District of Columbia's Board of Education. The charges were similar to those in the P.A.R.C. case, but since the site was in

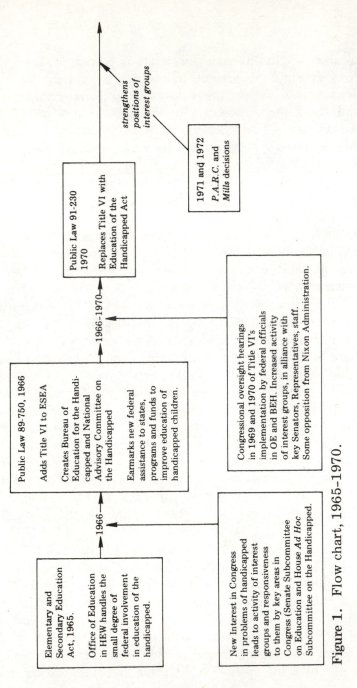

Figure 1. Flow chart, 1965–1970.

The following text appears within the flow chart:

Elementary and Secondary Education Act, 1965.

Office of Education in HEW handles the small degree of federal involvement in education of the handicapped.

New Interest in Congress in problems of handicapped leads to activity of interest groups and responsiveness to them by key areas in Congress (Senate Subcommittee on Education and House *Ad Hoc* Subcommittee on the Handicapped.

1966

Public Law 89-750, 1966

Adds Title VI to ESEA

Creates Bureau of Education for the Handicapped and National Advisory Committee on the Handicapped

Earmarks new federal assistance to states, programs and funds to improve education of handicapped children.

Congressional oversight hearings in 1969 and 1970 of Title VI's implementation by federal officials in OE and BEH. Increased activity of interest groups, in alliance with key Senators, Representatives, staff. Some opposition from Nixon Administration.

1966–1970

Public Law 91-230 1970

Replaces Title VI with Education of the Handicapped Act

1971 and 1972

P.A.R.C. and *Mills* decisions

strengthens positions of interest groups

the District of Columbia, any decision rendered by the Court could affect all federal jurisdictions. Between P.A.R.C. and Mills, therefore, the entire issue could be covered by court action. In August, 1972, in deciding for the parents and guardians, the Court ruled that under the 5th Amendment's due process of law clause every school age child in the District of Columbia shall be provided with ". . .a free and suitable publicly-supported education regardless of the degree of a child's mental, physical or emotional disability or impairment."

As the Congress began its oversight hearings in 1973, the right of a handicapped child to a publicly-supported education was now grounded in the Constitution. Due process, provided for by the 5th Amendment, and equal protection of the laws, provided by the 14th, as well as state public education laws and federal requirements for compulsory education, required a publicly-supported education be made available to *all* children. Henceforth, interest groups for handicapped children could argue constitutional and legal points as they sought to achieve more extensive programs and further federal funds for handicapped children by congressional enactment. The 1973-74 oversight hearings would bring about PL 93-830 as the scope of conflict widened. (See Figure 1.)

1973–1974: The Scope of Conflict Widens

Richard M. Nixon was re-elected to his second term as President in November 1972, carrying every state but Massachusetts and the District of Columbia. He received 47.17 million votes to George S. McGovern's 29.17 million, a majority of 60.99 per cent to the South Dakota Senator's 37.5 per cent. It was a stunning victory, and the Republican President took it as approval of the policies and programs initiated during his first four years and a mandate for the continuation of his leadership in his second term. Nixon had faced a Democratically-controlled Congress in both Congressional sessions from 1969 through 1972, and, despite his electoral sweep of the nation (he won 520 electoral votes), the Democrats again won a majority of seats in the 93rd Congress. The Democrats picked up two seats in the Senate for a total of 56 and retained 240 in the House (losing 15 from the total of 255 in the 92nd Congress). Thus, Nixon's legislative program would be presented to a relatively hostile Congress in 1973.

In his first term, Nixon had invoked Congressional displeasure with his continuation and escalation of the Vietnam war over the protests of members of both parties; his increasing use of impoundment (refusing to spend funds appropriated by Congress for various domestic projects); and, his claims that "executive privilege" exempted some of his top aides from testifying before Congressional committees. Nixon's behavior as President no doubt led to the passage of the War Powers Act (over his veto) and the Budget Reform and Impoundment Control Act by the newly elected Congress. But this, and the Watergate revelations, were yet to occur as Nixon now prepared to do battle with the first session of the 93rd Congress in 1973. The Senate and House committees of the 93rd Congress that dealt with matters of education remained substantially the same in 1973 as in the previous Congress.

The Labor and Public Welfare Committee[1] was essentially liberal in that most of its membership (both Democrats and Republicans) tended to favor increased federal assistance to education. In addition, there were no conservative Southern Democrats on the Committee (West Virginia and Maryland being considered border states). Only Republicans Dominick and Taft espoused the conservative view that the less the federal government "interfered" with the states and localities, the better. The liberals understood not only that the states and local communities were hard pressed to subsidize the increasing costs of education without substantial federal financial aid, but also that the requirements governing the use

---

[1]*Democrats 10*   *Republicans 6*

Harrison A. Williams, Jr. (NJ) *chairman*   Jacob K. Javits (NY)
Jennings Randolph (W Va)   Peter H. Dominick (Colo)
Claiborne Pell (RI)   Richard S. Schweiker (Pa)
Edward M. Kennedy (Mass)   Robert Taft, Jr. (Ohio)
Gaylord Nelson (Wis)   J. Glenn Beall, Jr. (Md)
Walter F. Mondale (Minn)   Robert T. Stafford (Vt)
Thomas Eagleton (Mo)
Alan Cranston (Calif)
Harold E. Hughes (Iowa)
William D. Hathaway (Maine) (new member in 1973)

of Federal funds could change the focus of education programs by dictating how the money *should be* spent and by mandating reports to the federal government as to how the money *had been* spent. Advocates of more federal aid and support for programs aimed at handicapped children, therefore, had a sympathetic ear in the Labor and Public Welfare Committee.

The Subcommittee on Education was chaired by Senator Claiborne Pell of Rhode Island and was composed of the full committee membership except for Nelson and Hughes, and Republican Taft. Thus, when the subcommittee came to support a particular position, or wrote its own bill emanating from its subcommittee hearings, it stood to reason that it spoke for the full committee. If interest groups could "bring the subcommittee around," in effect it had brought the full committee around. Since the Senate itself tends generally to accept the position of its committees on most matters, once the interest groups "reach" and "convince" the subcommittee of the legitimacy of their views, they have won their victories. The Education Subcommittee had written the Elementary and Secondary Education Act in 1965. Its highly skilled professional staff under two chairmanships had prepared the groundwork for the ESEA and carefully nurtured the subcommittee membership on the data and statistics which showed the crying need for more federal funds for the states so that they could upgrade their educational systems, particularly for the economically disadvantaged. The ESEA dovetailed with Lyndon B. Johnson's "war on poverty" and by 1973 was firmly entrenched as a national "institution."

The staff of the subcommittee was "spread thin," however, and federal aid to handicapped children was not receiving the full attention it deserved. In 1973, therefore, the Labor and Public Welfare Committee created a new Subcommittee on the Handicapped, seven Democrats and four Republicans.

The composition of the Subcommittee on Handicapped was practically the same as the Education Subcommittee. What was different, however, was the staff. A new staff was now free to spend *all* its time on one matter, education for the handicapped. Thus, when the professional staff of the Subcommittee on the Handicapped molded and shaped a new and broader bill for educating handicapped children with the ideas, aid, and support of the interest groups for the handicapped — and had that bill accepted by the Subcommittee on Handicapped, it was the same as having the full Senate accept it too.[2]

Constituency interests are often of paramount importance to any Senator or Member of the House. The Subcommittee on the Handicapped was no exception to that political rule. Four of the nine states which had more than an estimated 200,000 handicapped children (Texas, California, New York, Ohio, Michigan, Pennsylvania, Illinois, New Jersey and Missouri) were represented by one of their Senators on the Subcommittee for the Handicapped (California, Ohio, Pennsylvania and New Jersey). In addition, state aid for the education of the handicapped increased dramatically after the landmark *P.A.R.C.* and *Mills* decisions. As we can see from the following table, the activity in this area in each subcommittee member's state justified his support for in-

[2] *Senate Subcommittee on Education*

Democrats (8)	Republicans (5)
Pell, *Chairman*	Dominick
Randolph	Javits
Williams	Schweiker
Kennedy	Beall
Mondale	Stafford
Eagleton	
Cranston	
Hathaway	

Senate Subcommittee on Handicapped

Democrats(7)	Republicans (4)
Randolph, *Chairman*	Stafford
Cranston	Taft
Williams	Schweiker
Pell	Beall
Kennedy	
Mondale	
Hathaway	

creased Federal aid as well:

State Aid for the Education of the Handicapped
Increases FY 1972 — 1975

States	*FY 1972 ($)*	*FY 1975 ($)*	*%+*
West Virginia	2,004,208	4,633,525	31.2
California	154,009,596	320,300,000	107.9
New Jersey	41,965,000	76,702,930	28.8
Rhode Island	13,500,000	16,500,000	22.2
Massachusetts	18,120,250	47,080,379	159.8
Minnesota	18,633,000	28,500,000	53.0
Maine	1,352,615	6,500,000	381.0
Vermont	2,069,576	4,396,000	112.4
Ohio	66,245,828	103,046,565	56.1
Pennsylvania	81,403,000	168,000,000	106.4
Maryland	27,066,000	42,715,000	57.8

Political and constituency interest, therefore, coupled with philosophical agreement, served to strengthen the position of the Labor and Public Welfare Committee on the issue of education for handicapped children. Interest groups involved in this issue were not unaware of the connection.

HOUSE, 93RD CONGRESS, 1973-1974, EDUCATION AND LABOR COMMITTEE

The House Committee on Education and Labor, unlike its counterpart in the Senate, was not as completely committed to the "liberal" view on education matters. Being a larger committee than the Senate Labor and Public Welfare Committee (22 Democrats and 16 Republicans), it had a broader perspective with stronger representation of basic conservatism, particularly among the Republicans. The Committee was chaired by Carl Perkins of Kentucky, who had taken over the leadership from Adam Clayton Powell of New York in January, 1967. Eighteen of the 22 Democrats were holdovers from the previous Congress as were 13 of the 16 Republicans. The more populated and more urban-oriented states had a preponderance of members of the committee (New York, 5, New Jersey, 3, California, 3 and Pennsylvania, 3). The Democratic side also had a "non-Southern" bent, and eight of the nine States with substantial numbers of handicapped children had Representatives on the full committee. Only Texas did not.[3]

Two important subcommittees of the House Education and Labor Committee had jurisdiction over matters relating to the handicapped: the Subcommittee on General Education, chaired by Perkins (who also chaired the full committee), and the Subcommittee on Select Education, chaired by Brademas. The latter subcommittee was the heir to the original *Ad Hoc* Subcommittee on the Handicapped which, under the chairmanship of Hugh Carey (D-NY), had estab-

[3] *Democrats (22)*   *Republicans (16)*

Carl D. Perkins (D Ky.), *Chairman*
Frank Thompson Jr. (N.J.)   Albert H. Quie (Minn.)
John H. Dent (Pa.)   John M. Ashbrook (Ohio)
Dominick V. Daniels (N.J.)   Alphonzo Bell (Calif.)
John Brademas (Ind.)   John N. Erlenborn (Ill.)
James G. O'Hara (Mich.)   John Dellenback (Ore.)
Augustus F. Hawkins (Calif.)   Marvin L. Esch (Mich.)
William D. Ford (Mich.)   Edwin D. Eshleman (Pa.)
Patsy T. Mink (Hawaii)   William A. Steiger (Wis.)
Lloyd Meeds (Wash.)   Earl F. Landgrebe (Ind.)
Philip Burton (Calif.)   Orval Hansen (Idaho)
Joseph M. Gaydos (Pa.)   Edwin B. Forsythe (N.J.)
William (Bill) Clay (Mo.)   Jack F. Kemp (N.Y.)
Shirley Chisholm (N.Y.)   Peter A. Peyser (N.Y.)
Mario Biaggi (N.Y.)   David Towell (Nev.)
Ella T. Grasso (Conn.)   Ronald A. Sarasin (Conn.)
Romano L. Mazzoli (Ky.)   Robert J. Huber (Mich.)
Herman Badillo (N.Y.)
Ike F. Andrews (N.C.)
William Lehman (Fla.)
Jaime Benitez (P.R.)
Vacancy

lished the first base in the House for the handicapped advocacy groups in 1966.

The Republicans on both Subcommittees leaned towards the conservative side, and six of the eight Democrats on the Select Education Subcommittee were also on the General Education Subcommittee.[4]

President Nixon's "Better Schools Act" Proposal, 1973.

In March, 1973, Nixon's educational proposals were outlined for the House Subcommittee on General Education by Caspar W. Weinberger, Secretary of the Department of Health, Education and Welfare. Drawing on Nixon's theme as expressed in the President's 1973 State of the Union Message, Weinberger stressed that the President's goal for education was in keeping with his views on the "new federalism." In Nixon's words. . .

> Rather than stifling initiative by trying to direct everything from Washington, Federal efforts should encourage State and local governments to make those decisions and supply those services for which their closeness to the people best qualifies them.

[4]

Subcommittee on General Education		Subcommittee on Select Education	
Democrats (11)	*Republicans (6)*	*Democrats (8)*	*Republicans (5)*
Perkins, Chair (Ky)	Bell (Calif.)	Brademas, Chair (Ind.)	Eshleman (Pa.)
Meeds (Wash.)	Ashbrook (Ohio)	Mink (Hawaii)	Landgrebe (Ind.)
Ford (Mich.)	Forsythe (N.J.)	Meeds (Wash.)	Hansen (Idaho)
Hawkins (Calif.)	Peyser (N.Y.)	Chisholm (N.Y.)	Peyser (N.Y.)
Mink (Hawaii)	Teiger (Wis.)	Grasso (Conn.)	Sarasin (Conn.)
Chisholm (N.Y.)	Towell (Nev.)	Mazzoli (Ky.)	
Biaggi (N.Y.)		Badillo (N.Y.)	
Mazzoli (Ky.)		Lehman (Fla.)	
Badillo (N.Y.)			
Lehman (Fla.)			
Andrews (N.C.)			

The President then had gone on to say. . .

> 1973 must be a year of decisive action to restructure
> Federal aid programs for education. Our goal is to pro-
> vide continued Federal financial support for our schools
> *while expanding State and local control over basic edu-*
> *cational decisions.* (Italics added.)[5]

By 1973, those advocating increased federal aid for educating handicapped children did not want to expand state
and local control over expenditures of funds without ensuring by federal law that those funds would be carefully and
thoughtfully spent. They had not labored for passage of the
ESEA amendments in 1966 and for increased funds after that
only to see the states and local school districts able to "fritter
away" federal monies without paying heed to the deficiencies
inherent in the local system. The handicapped interest groups
were well aware of the tendency of states and local school
districts to short-change handicapped children. Only by holding the localities to strict compliance with federal law and the
Constitution could they hope to have handicapped children
educated as fully as possible. If the *P.A.R.C.* and *Mills*
decisions meant anything, they were a warning to the States
that they would be forced either by litigation (costly to
handicapped interest groups as well as states) or by increased
pressure for federal requirements to adhere to the principle
that handicapped children were *entitled* to a free, appropriate
public education. President Nixon's approach was not com-
patible with this view.

The handicapped interest groups were particularly concerned that Nixon's views of revenue-sharing would do
irreparable harm to the progress they had made by 1973.
Nixon's "Better Schools Act" (H.R. 5823 and S. 1319)

---

[5] Quoted in *Hearings on Elementary and Secondary Education
Amendments of 1973*, Subcommittee on General Education of House
Committee on Education and Labor, Part 2, 93rd Congress, 1st Session,
1973, p. 1794.

would have completely redefined the federal role in education by consolidating the various categorical grant programs in education (32 in number) into one single revenue-sharing program. Nixon proposed to create five broad categories — aid for the educationally disadvantaged, impact aid for school districts containing an abundance of children of those employed in federal positions, vocational education, education of the handicapped, and aid for support services. Such an approach flew in the face of what interest groups for the handicapped had been fighting for — recognition of handicapped children as entitled to special, very special, attention being paid to them by both federal and state governments. That was the reason for their arguing for the creation of the Bureau of Education for the Handicapped (BEH) in the first place, and they continued to press for a more comprehensive program. If Nixon's "Better Schools Act" was enacted, not only would the states and school districts be able to return to the days of neglect of the handicapped (for the handicapped interest groups assumed that the local school districts would not be willing to place emphasis on handicapped children who were a small proportion of other children in each district), but also attempts to secure more and more federal funds for education of handicapped children would be lost in the scurry for federal aid for all educational purposes. The creation of a Senate Subcommittee on the Handicapped was symbolic. Handicapped children were a very special group and had to be treated that way by the Congress and the Administration.

Nixon's proposal, furthermore, would have permitted a state to transfer up to 30 per cent of its allocated federal funds for vocational *and* handicapped education and 100 per cent of the supporting services funds it received to any other area except impact aid. If Congress were to enact that into law, the handicapped groups knew very well what would happen in most of the states. Education for the handicapped necessitated complete "services support" (transportation, payments for orthopedic devices, counseling etc.). To allow the states and school districts to siphon those funds away from the handicapped would undercut everything that had been accomplished so far and place severe obstacles in the way of further strides for educating the handicapped. It would do little good to have the courts say the handicapped children were entitled to a free, appropriate public education if there were few funds set aside to do it.

Fortunately for the handicapped interest groups, Nixon was by 1973 in disrepute in the Congress. The House Subcommittee on General Education was not about to pay the Nixon proposals much heed, and its membership was unsympathetic to the President's proposals in general. In 1973, the Senate and House took up their own versions of ESEA, with education for the handicapped still treated as a special concern.

Handicapped Legislation in 1973-1974

Public Law 91-230, which created the Education of the Handicapped Act previously discussed, was due to expire on June 30, 1973. Written into the act was an automatic extension of one year in the event that the Congress failed to pass a re-authorization measure by that time. The Congress, therefore, was due to conduct oversight hearings into the implementation of PL 91-230 and to deal with various bills proposed in the field of education for the handicapped in 1973. Because the Congress had the leeway of one extra year, it could take its time both overseeing past performances of the federal and state governments and holding hearings on new proposals and new ideas.

The situation in 1973 can be examined with an eye for the complications of the legislative process. Nixon's "Better Schools Act" — the President's view — was proposed to the House in H.R. 5823 by Congressman Bell of California, one of the ranking Republicans on the House Education and Labor Committee. A Presidential measure can be introduced in the Congress only by a Senator or Representative. It is the usual custom for a member of the President's party who sits on the committee having jurisdiction over the content of the President's proposal to introduce the bill on behalf of the President, or "by request." The "by request" — which is inserted in the language of the introduction of the bill — signifies that the bill is not essentially that of the one formally introducing it. H.R. 5823 fell into this category. The President's bill was also introduced on the Senate side as S. 1319 by Senator Dominick of Colorado, a ranking Republican on the Senate Labor and Public Welfare Committee, and although not a "by request" bill, it was not given high priority by the Senate Committee.

An important point should be made here about this legislative process. We often take for granted that the President is the "legislative leader" of the Congress in that he sets his legislative priorities by the importance he places on his legislative proposals. Thus the Congress responds and reacts to his proposals by rejecting or passing them after extensive Committee alterations. True enough, but on any legislative issue, particular members of the Senate and the House, usually members of the Committee having jurisdiction over that specific type of issue, also put *their* versions into the legislative hopper. Thus, the Committee or Subcommittees having jurisdiction often have several bills before them — the President's (indirectly) and those introduced by the Committee (or other) members.

Once an issue has been at least partially resolved by an Act of Congress, a Department or administrative agency (for example, the Health, Education and Welfare Department, Bureau of Education for the Handicapped, or Office of Education) implements the law after having written and published the regulations under the statute. As time passes, however, particularly when the Public Law must be reauthorized in due time by the Congress, the relationship tightens among the interest groups involved in the substance of the law, the Congressional committee members *and their staffs* having legislative jurisdiction over the law and the federal agency officers charged with administering the law. This is the so-called "iron triangle." So it was with the Education of the Handicapped legislation in 1973. (See Figure 2.)

Recall that the foothold for legislation on education of the handicapped was the Elementary and Secondary Education Act of 1965. ESEA of 1965 did very little in the field of education for handicapped children. In 1966 the Congress amended the ESEA of 1965 by passing S. 3406 (PL 89-750) which inserted a new Title VI, a section devoted to upgrading the education of handicapped children through

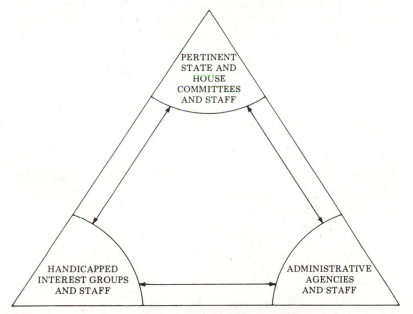

Figure 2. Iron Triangle: Legislation for Education of the Handicapped.

the creation of BEH. Then, in 1970, the Congress further committed itself to involvement of the federal government with passage of PL 91-230, the Education of the Handicapped Act, which repealed Title VI of ESEA and created a separate act, the Education of the Handicapped Act, which authorized state grants for the improvement of state programs for educating handicapped children. The separation and expansion of Federal aid to the handicapped was a positive response to the needs of the handicapped represented by their interest groups.

The Congress was due to legislate re-authorizations of both ESEA of 1965 (as amended) and the Education of the Handicapped Act in 1973. It should be remembered that the ESEA of 1965 was primarily a federal program to upgrade educational opportunities for economically disadvantaged children by supplying federal funds to the states for compensatory educational services. President Nixon's bills (H.R. 5823 and S. 1319) were an attempt to combine the principles of the ESEA and the Education of the Handicapped Act into one legislative entity. The Nixon Administration had linked them as part of Nixon's program to restructure federal aid to the states for education into an over-all revenue-sharing plan. (The concept was totally unacceptable to the groups representing handicapped children.)

H.R. 5823 was assigned in the House to the Subcommittee on General Education, chaired by Carl Perkins, who was also the chairman of the full Education and Labor Committee. The Subcommittee also had before it three other education bills, introduced very early in the 1973 session:

1. H.R. 16, introduced by Perkins himself, was essentially a "financial act" for educational grants to the states.
2. H.R. 69, also introduced by Perkins, was the major bill the Committee would use in its hearings and would be the vehicle used in the House. H.R. 69 was the re-authorization of the ESEA — a broadly con-

strued education bill — which contained within it
(Title I, Section 111) the extension of the Education
of the Handicapped Act for four fiscal years.
3. H.R. 5163, introduced by Albert H. Quie, the ranking
Republican on the House Education and Labor Committee, although not a member of the Subcommittee
on General Education, was his version for reauthorizing ESEA. It was an omnibus education bill
making only passing reference to educating handicapped children but including some authorization for
federal support to the states.

The other side of the double-pronged approach of the
House toward educating handicapped children was in the
House Subcommittee on Select Education, chaired by John
Brademas. He had introduced H.R. 4199, which would have
extended the Education of the Handicapped Act for three
fiscal years at a fairly high level of federal funds. Since the
Subcommittee on General Education would be concerned
with *all* federal programs in education (including education
for handicapped children), Brademas' Subcommittee on
Select Education could devote its (*and its staff's*) full time to
hearing out the issues through consideration of his H.R.
4199. It was not necessary to enact H.R. 4199 immediately
but it was politically and legislatively necessary to set the
stage with a solid base for future enactments.

Groups advocating greater involvement of the federal government and more financial aid in the field of educating
handicapped children thus had two House subcommittees
open to them; the House Subcommittee on General Education and the House Subcommittee on Select Education. The
former was considering extension of the Education of the
Handicapped Act, the latter was concentrating on it.

Bicameralism — a two-house legislative system — offers
double opportunity for spreading the views of the people,
through their interest groups, on the public record. In the
area of education, the Senate was doing the same thing as the

House, with an even stronger emphasis on examining the needs of handicapped children. The interest groups could now reinforce their positions before the appropriate Senate subcommittees.

Claiborne Pell, chairman of the Senate Subcommittee on Education, introduced S. 1539. Like its House companion, H.R. 69, Pell's bill authorized the extension of the ESEA and also contained a provision (Title III) extending the Education of the Handicapped Act for three more fiscal years. Pell's Subcommittee was assigned S. 1539. S. 1319, the Senate counterpart to Nixon's House bill (H.R. 5823) was introduced in the Senate by Senator Dominick, the ranking Republican on the Subcommittee on Education, and was also assigned to the same subcommittee. An indication of the lack of interest by the subcommittee in Nixon's proposals, however, can be seen on the cover of each of the seven parts of the subcommittee's hearings on S. 1539 and S. 1319. Instead of printing both numbers of the proposals on the cover, the Subcommittee printed only S. 1539 "and related bills." The subcommittee was indeed making a point. It would center its investigation on *its* bill, not the President's, whose views simply held no priority for the subcommittee.

Since the Senate Labor and Public Welfare Committee had created a new Subcommittee on the Handicapped in 1973 (with yet another professional staff), it was naturally intent on studying in great detail the issue of education for handicapped children on its own. The Subcommittee on the Handicapped, chaired by Senator Jennings Randolph, now had before it four bills dealing specifically with the expansion of the federal role in educating handicapped children. Thus while one Senate subcommittee (Education) held hearings on the ESEA (just as the House Subcommittee on General Education was doing), another Senate subcommittee (on The Handicapped) could direct its attention specifically to problems of handicapped children (just as the House Committee on Select Education was also doing). And, most importantly for the handicapped, two important avenues of access were thus opened to them.

The Senate Subcommittee on the Handicapped had the following bills before it in 1973:

1. S. 896, introduced by Subcommittee Chairman Jennings Randolph, would have extended the Education of the Handicapped Act for three more fiscal years and upgraded the importance of the Bureau of Education for the Handicapped by adding four more senior positions to it.
2. S. 34, introduced by Senator Ernest Hollings of South Carolina, who was not a member of the Labor and Public Welfare Committee, was designed to include federal funds for research in the problems of autistic children.
3. S. 808, introduced by Senator Mike Gravel of Alaska, who was not a member of the Labor and Public Welfare Committee, was a bill supplying federal funds to screen elementary school children in order to identify children with specific learning disabilities.
4. S. 6, introduced by Harrison Williams, chairman of Labor and Public Welfare Committee, was a comprehensive bill for educating handicapped children taking into account the *P.A.R.C.* and *Mills* decisions. It would have mandated by law the availability of a free appropriate public education to all handicapped children 1976.

THE HEARINGS AND THE IRON TRIANGLE — 1973-1974

To understand how a bill becomes a law, it is necessary to comprehend the labyrinth of the congressional system. By 1973, as we have explained, the scope of conflict over education of the handicapped legislation had widened a great deal, bringing into the legislative picture more subcommittees, more staff and more pressures from groups representing handicapped children. In addition, the creation of the BEH within the Office of Education had given the groups and the congressional subcommittees and staff a more firmly imbedded root in the Administration. Because PL 91-230 was to expire on June 30, 1973, the Congress somehow had to write new legislation extending its life and, at the same time, increasing the kind and amount of federal aid to the states for education in general and the handicapped in particular. Being granted that extra year, until June 30, 1974, because of the automatic extension of one year in PL 91-230, the Congress took its time in weaving together a new law, called the Omnibus Education Act, which contained the extension of the ESEA and the Education of the Handicapped Act. This act went into effect on August 21, 1974 when President Ford signed the measure. Between January, 1973 and August 1974, a great deal happened in the legislative process to produce the Omnibus Education Act. After explaining the chronology of education legislation in 1973 and 1974, we shall then go into the specific role that the interest groups played in passage of the Omnibus Education Act (PL 93-380) in interacting with the Congress and the Administration.

CHRONOLOGY OF LEGISLATION

The Senate Subcommittee on Education held extensive hearings on S. 1539, Senator Pell's comprehensive bill extending the life of ESEA. These hearings began in April, 1973 and ended in October, 1973, without any significant testimony being given by interest groups for the handicapped. They concentrated their attention and efforts on the newly-created Senate Subcommittee on the Handicapped, which had jurisdiction in this area. Separating the problems of handicapped children from the overall approach to education as embodied in S. 1539 was convenient for the Senate too. Thus on March 20, 21 and 23, 1973 the groups made their case to the Senate in hearings conducted by the Subcommittee on the Handicapped on S. 896. The Senate handled the inclusion of legislation for the handicapped in S. 1539 this way. After the Subcommittee on the Handicapped concluded its hearings on S. 896, the Labor and Public Welfare Committee, its parent committee, reported it out to the Senate favorably on June 21, 1973. Four days later, June 25, 1973, the Senate passed S. 896 — now called the Education of the Handicapped Amendments of 1973 — by a voice vote. However, the House companion bill had been included in its version of Education Amendments of 1974. Therefore the Senate Subcommittee on the Handicapped made S. 896 Title IV of S. 1539, the Senate version of ESEA reauthorization, and it was reported as such by the Senate Labor and Public Welfare Committee on March 29, 1974. S. 1539, which now included the language of S. 896, awaited action by the full Senate.

On the House side, the Subcommittee on General Education held its hearings on H.R. 69 (and the other related bills) beginning in January, 1973 and ending in June, 1973. In the meantime, matters of education for handicapped children were being investigated by John Brademas' Subcommittee on Select Education which held hearings on Brademas' H.R. 4199 on March 9 and 21, 1973. (Thus, during the month of March, 1973, groups representing the interests of the handicapped could testify before the Senate Subcommittee on the Handicapped and the House Subcommittee on Select Education.) By the end of March, 1973 they had finished getting on the public record the conditions of handicapped children in the states and their views for more federal aid. The House Education and Labor Committee, the parent body to the Subcommittee on General Education and the Subcommittee on Select Education, then took the provisions of H.R. 4199 and included a section on education for the handicapped in its favorable report to the House on H.R. 69, nearly one year later, on February 5, 1974. On March 27, 1974, The House passed H.R. 69 by a vote of 380-26. On May 20, 1974, the Senate passed S. 1539 by a vote of 81-5. The House and Senate then went to conference to iron out the differences between the two bills. The conference report cleared the Congress on August 7, 1974 and was signed into law on August 21, 1974. Although the federal role had continued to be one of encouragement and support of state efforts, PL 93-380 included a large increase in financial aid with a one year authorization to assist states in meeting the new responsibilities outlined in the act. Responsibilities of the states included: identifying and evaluating handicapped children, developing a policy for educating handicapped children and a timetable for meeting this goal, and establishing due process and confidentiality in order to guarantee fairness in deciding the extent of services to handicapped children.

The Senate Subcommittee on the Handicapped continued its work on S. 6, a more extensive approach to the entire issue. The new requirements and authorizations for fiscal year 1975 represented a clear mandate for the development of a more comprehensive piece of legislation and for a more active Federal role in this area. Looking towards 1975, and the new 94th Congress, therefore, the Senate Subcommittee on the Handicapped conducted hearings on S. 6 between April, 1973 and June, 1974. On the House side, the Subcommittee on Select Education conducted hearings on a similar bill, Brademas' H.R. 70, in March, 1974. Both bills would form the basis for a new beginning in 1975.

CONGRESSIONAL HEARINGS: 1973

The educational community in Washington (particularly the interest groups and the Sentate and House education committees and their staffs) generally believed that the Nixon Administration was impeding the will of the Congress by dragging its feet in implementing the provisions of the Education of the Handicapped Act created by PL 91-230. Although the Bureau of Education for the Handicapped had supported the development of programs for handicapped children in a forthright manner, it appeared to suffer under excessive political dominance of the Office of Education. In addition, transfer of several education programs for the handicapped to the BEH was slow in coming. Personnel freezes and the mentality of suspicion seemingly inherent in the Nixon Administration hindered the effectiveness of the BEH. It was the only major unit in OE with but one super-grade position. In the view of Senator Jennings Randolph, chairman of the newly-created Subcommittee on the Handi-capped, the BEH's 110 person staff needed "beefing up." To reaffirm his and the Senate Subcommittee's belief that there had to be a "strong identifiable administrative organization within the Office of Education" if federal programs for the handicapped were "to be coordinated rather than isolated,"[6] Senator Randolph had introduced S. 896 in February, 1973.

Randolph's bill would have created four new super-grade (GS 16) assistants to the Director of the BEH, thereby giving the Bureau some administrative muscle. S. 896 also autho-rized continuation of the Education of the Handicapped Act for three more years with increased federal funds for state grants for education programs for the handicapped, special centers and services, teacher education, research and demon-stration projects, education media services, research in teach-ing children with specific learning disabilities, and aid in locating handicapped children. In addition, S. 896 also con-tinued the National Advisory Committee on Handicapped Children and required the Director of the BEH to report directly to the Commissioner of Education.

[6] Senate Report, No. 93-238, *Education of the Handicapped Amendments of 1973.* 93rd Cong., 1st Sess., June 21, 1973, p. 6.

The other major bill Randolph's Committee was considering was S. 6, introduced in January 1973 by Harrison Williams, Jr., Chairman of the Labor and Public Welfare Committee and number two ranking Democrat on the Subcommittee on the Handicapped. Williams wanted a very broad and comprehensive bill to support education of handicapped children. For one thing, the bill was so constructed that by 1976 states would have to guarantee to all handicapped children a "free appropriate public education," in line with the *P.A.R.C.* and *Mills* decisions that handicapped children were indeed so entitled. Stringent requirements were listed by S. 6 for the states in order for them to receive federal funds, which were designated as supplementary to state funds and not to be used to supplant state funds. By 1973, 40 states had some sort of legislation for handicapped children, although not all state programs were mandated. If the *P.A.R.C.* and *Mills* decisions set any sort of precedent, however, the states would eventually have to supply appropriate educational services to their handicapped children. It was in their interest to get some Federal assistance to fulfill these mandates. With federal assistance, however, came federal regulation. And, S. 6 had plenty of that.

To be eligible for federal funds under S. 6, first, the state had to have an effective plan that assured all handicapped children the right to a "free, appropriate public education." Second, the state had to establish a plan which detailed the steps which would be taken to make that education available within three years, develop a timetable for accomplishing that goal, and provide the necessary facilities, personnel, and services. Third, the state had to demonstrate to the federal government it was making adequate progress in meeting its own timetable. Fourth, the state had to see to it that each local educational agency maintained a detailed and individualized program for each handicapped child, reviewed that program annually, and came into agreement with the parents or guardians of the handicapped child. The states had to assure due process procedures throughout the program, with all the protections and requirements of written notices that are part of due process. Fifth, the states had to abide by non-discriminatory procedures in classifying handicapped children to avoid racial or cultural bias. Sixth, the states had to "mainstream" their handicapped children in regular classrooms, which required extensive "retraining" of regular teachers. Seventh, the states had to establish advisory panels to advise the state educational agencies of "unmet needs" of handicapped children. Eighth, the states had to supply the same services for handicapped children who were enrolled in private schools as in public schools. Ninth, the states could not use federal funds to supplant their own state and local funds. Federal funds could ·only be used as a supplement, thereby forcing the states and local educational agencies to establish handicapped programs with their own money *first*. Tenth, the states had to embark on a program to find and identify every handicapped child in the states. The applications for federal assistance would of course be detailed, and all the plans and programs subject to federal evaluation.

S. 896 and S. 6, together with S. 808 (Gravel's bill on "specific learning disabilities") and S. 34 (Hollings' bill on problems of autistic children) constituted the basis for the March, 1973 Senate hearings on the needs of handicapped children. In the same month, on the other side of Capitol Hill, the House Subcommittee on Select Education, under the chairmanship of John Brademas, held its hearings on H.R. 4199.

THE SENATE HEARINGS, 1973

The Senate Subcommittee on the Handicapped was well aware of the Nixon Administration's opposition to the general approaches being taken by S. 896 and S. 6. Caspar W. Weinberger, then Secretary of Health, Education and Welfare, flatly rejected S. 896's purpose of legislatively mandating grade levels below "the highest administrative levels." Weinberger also stated that the provisions of S. 6 requiring strict state compliance with certain practices in order to receive federal funds were "inconsistent with the Administration's policy of placing greater control of Federal resources in the hands of State and local citizens."[7] The Senate subcommittee, however, paid little attention to the Nixon Administration which by then had lost most of its credibility with the Congress, as well as most of the nation. The Subcommittee went full speed ahead with its intention to legitimize its comprehensive approach to educate the nation's handicapped children.

The Subcommittee's hearings involved testimony from more than 45 witnesses representing about 20 interest groups representing the handicapped. But new participants emerged as the hearings progressed. Testimony was now coming from more and more state and local educational agencies, as well as other interest groups of government, an indication of new recognition of the effects of this legislation on the states. Government interest groups had always been interacting agents with the federal government on several matters including education for the economically disadvantaged and federal "impact aid." However, the federal assistance programs for the handicapped had not required such interaction on the part of state and local education agencies before. Hearings on these early federal initiatives had been dominated by groups representing beneficiaries of handicapped programs. But, the tide was running the other way in Congress now and, since the courts had ruled that education for the handicapped was a rights issue, agencies which provided services at all levels were affected by new programs. The scope of conflict had widened and groups representing state and local governments

---

[7]Caspar W. Weinberger to Harrison A. Williams, Jr., April 2, 1973, quoted in Senate Report 93-238, *ibid.*, p. 25.

now presented the views of their constituencies at hearings dealing with programs for the handicapped.

A theme ran through the testimony of the handicapped groups.[8] One, they looked with suspicion on the revenue-sharing programs that had become fashionable in some quarters in the early 1970's, fearing that this approach — which gave a great deal of discretion to the states in spending their revenue-sharing money — meant that handicapped children would come out at the bottom of the list, "left out as usual." Therefore, they pressed for the continuation of federal assistance along more familiar lines; through federal categorized grants administered by the BEH. Two, they argued for extension of the Education of the Handicapped Act for three more years so that they could evaluate over a long period of time the implementation of the Act and the effect of the actual appropriations (always lower than the authorizations) eventually expended on handicapped programs. Third, although the data and statistical evaluations were hazy, they wanted to ensure that only excess costs would be covered by federal assistance. The interest groups feared that unless this was regulated closely the states would substitute federal funds for state funds, instead of adding more to the handicapped slice of the education pie.

The Nixon Administration, however, was trying to scuttle the approach Congress had been taking to educate handicapped children. Committed to a lesser role for the federal government in the lives of Americans, Nixon's approach was to permit the states to do more on their own responsibility, using federal money but without strict federal supervision.

---

[8] Among the groups testifying before the Subcommittee on the Handicapped were the National Association for Autistic Children; the National Federation of the Blind; the American Foundation of the Blind; the Council for Exceptional Children, the National Association for Retarded Children; the United Cerebral Palsy Association; the American Speech and Hearing Association; the Council on Education of the Deaf; and the National Center on Media and Materials.

HEW sent its Assistant Secretary for Legislation, Stephen Kurzman, to the Senate subcommittee hearings to lobby for that position. Although agreeing that much progress had been made under the Education of the Handicapped Act, Kurzman argued that the nation would be better served if *all* educational assistance to the states were consolidated into Nixon's revenue-sharing plan. Nixon's idea was to turn decision-making as to how to spend federal funds back to the states. The Administration did not want to continue the system of having the federal government's BEH approve state plans *beforehand*, but only to monitor the programs after the fact.[9]

The Senate Subcommittee did not sympathize with the Administration plan. Preferring its own method as outlined by S. 896 and S. 6, the Subcommittee generally ignored Nixon's proposal, the "Better Schools Act" of 1973. Federal financial assistance and federal inducements to the states, by requiring them to present plans before receiving funds and have those plans approved first, had been catalysts to the states' developing programs for their handicapped children. Without earmarking funds, which revenue-sharing threatened, the states would place education for handicapped children lower down on their list of priorities. The handicapped interest groups, too, took issue with the Nixon Administration, claiming that only with federal financial support and federal guidelines that were strictly enforced could education for handicapped children make more headway. By 1973 about 400 colleges and universities, using federal grant money, were preparing special education teachers, a tenfold increase in the last twenty years. But even with 40 states having some sort of mandatory legislation for education of handicapped children by 1973, 7 states educated fewer than

[9]*Hearings, Education for the Handicapped Act, 1973*, S. 896, S. 6., S. 34 and S. 808 Senate Subcommittee on the Handicapped, Committee on Labor and Public Welfare, 93rd Congress, 1st Sess., March 20, 21 and 23, pp. 443-449.

20 per cent of their *known* handicapped (the manner of identification of handicapped still had not been perfected), 1 state fewer than 10 per cent, and those states with the best record only about 70 per cent.[10]

More and better teachers — about 200,000 to 300,000 — were still needed if the full commitment to educate handicapped children were to become a reality. Only continued federal involvement and federal guidance would move the nation along those lines.

On June 21, 1973 the Senate Labor and Public Welfare Committee unanimously reported out S. 896 favorably with Randolph's original proposals intact. The Senate Subcommittee on the Handicapped would continue to investigate the provisions of S. 6, ending hearings in June, 1974, after visiting Newark, Boston, Columbia, St. Paul and Harrisburg. Thus, the Subcommittee could begin a new set of hearings in the 94th Congress, 1975, with a firm foundation of opinions written into the public record of 1974. S. 896 gave the representatives the handicapped pretty much what they wanted at the time — continued special recognition, increased funds, greater importance and prestige of the BEH, more pressures on the states to do their part in order to receive federal funds, and the legitimacy of their educational goals, in particular the statutory recognition of the constitutional right of a handicapped child to a "free appropriate public education." S. 896 was placed before the full Senate and passed by voice vote on June 25, 1973.

THE HOUSE HEARINGS — 1973

In the same month as the Senate Subcommittee on the Handicapped held its hearings on S. 6 and S. 896, so too did the House Subcommittee on Select Education hold its hearings on Brademas' bill, H.R. 4199. The hearings were short

[10] *Ibid.*, p. 469.

and to the point with Brademas, the Subcommittee Chairman, stressing that it was his and the subcommittee's intention to press for federal support for the education of the handicapped "without disruption."[11] The Council for Exceptional Children led the hearings on the first day with its usual clear analysis of where handicapped children stood in fiscal 1972. The testimony of its representatives emphasized that the percent of funds expended by each of the states for special education in fiscal 1972 varied from a low of 1.05 per cent of total state education expenditures (Arkansas) to a high of 8.4 per cent of total state education expenditures (Connecticut). From a state by state comparison, it was clear that the poorer states expended two to three times *less* in percentage of total state education expenditures than the wealthier states. The number of handicapped children in the nation was about 6.6 million (estimated), but in fiscal 1972, despite increased interest of and aid from the federal government, only 39 per cent of those 6.6 million were being served. The range of services by the states varied from a low of 8 per cent (North Dakota) to highs of 81, 75, 71 and 70 per cent (Washington, Florida, Illinois and Minnesota, respectively).

Stressing the potential "loss in the shuffle" if handicapped programs and funds ceased to be earmarked and were meshed with revenue-sharing, as Nixon wanted, the Council for Exceptional Children pleaded for more money and clearer delineation of authority for the BEH. H.R. 4199 was endorsed also by the United Cerebral Palsy Association, National Center for Law and the Handicapped, American Speech and Hearing Association, Council on Education of the Deaf, National Association for Retarded Children, National Easter Seal Society for Crippled Children and Adults, National Society for Autistic Children, and National

---

[11] Hearings, *Education of the Handicapped Act Amendments*, H.R. 4199, House Subcommittee on Select Education, House Education and Labor Committee, 93rd. Cong., 1st sess., March 9 and 21, 1973, p. 2.

Therapeutic Recreation Society. They all lauded the BEH's work, under the leadership of Dr. Edwin Martin, Jr. for its efforts on behalf of handicapped children and urged increased congressional commitment. HEW's Stephen Kurzman put forth the Nixon view of revenue-sharing, just as he was to do a short time later before the Senate Subcommittee on the Handicapped. But it was obvious the House subcommittee thought no better of it than would the Senate subcommittee. If the nation was to upgrade its efforts to educate handicapped children, the Federal government would have to distribute a greater share of federal revenues to state and local educational agencies. The leadership for this principle was coming not from the Administration, but from the Congress.

PUBLIC LAW 93-380: THE EDUCATION AMENDMENTS OF 1974

The Senate Labor and Public Welfare Committee incorporated S. 896 (which had already passed the Senate) into its version of S. 1539 because the House Education and Labor Committee had incorporated similar provisions of S. 896 into its H.R. 69, making these provisions conferenceable. The Senate and House went into joint conference committee (as previously explained in the chronology) to bring together their differing views on the elementary and secondary education programs. The Senate and House had no disagreement on the Education of the Handicapped section in both S. 1539 and H.R. 69. The upshot was passage of the Education Amendments of 1974, which in one Act re-authorized the Elementary and Secondary Education Act of 1965 (as amended) and the Education of the Handicapped Act which had been previously enacted in 1970. On August 21, 1974, twelve days after assuming the Presidency following Nixon's resignation on August 9, President Gerald Ford signed the measure into PL 93-380.

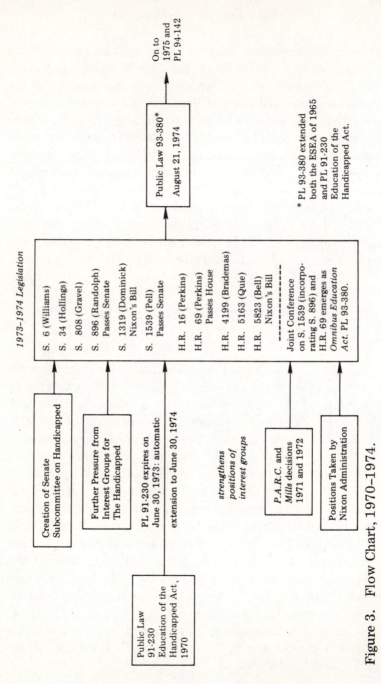

Figure 3. Flow Chart, 1970–1974.

1973–1974 Legislation

Public Law 91-230 Education of the Handicapped Act, 1970

Creation of Senate Subcommittee on Handicapped

Further Pressure from Interest Groups for The Handicapped

PL 91-230 expires on June 30, 1973: automatic extension to June 30, 1974

S. 6 (Williams)
S. 34 (Hollings)
S. 808 (Gravel)
S. 896 (Randolph) Passes Senate
S. 1319 (Dominick) Nixon's Bill
S. 1539 (Pell) Passes Senate

H.R. 16 (Perkins)
H.R. 69 (Perkins) Passes House
H.R. 4199 (Brademas)
H.R. 5163 (Quie)
H.R. 5823 (Bell) Nixon's Bill

Joint Conference on S. 1539 (incorporating S. 896) and H.R. 69 emerges as *Omnibus Education Act.* PL 93-380.

strengthens positions of interest groups

P.A.R.C. and *Mills* decisions 1971 and 1972

Positions Taken by Nixon Administration

Public Law 93-380* August 21, 1974

On to 1975 and PL 94-142

* PL 93-380 extended both the ESEA of 1965 and PL 91-230 Education of the Handicapped Act.

The Federal involvement with education for handicapped children was now contained in Title VI, Part B, Sections 611 through 621 of PL 93-380, known as the "Education of the Handicapped Amendments of 1974." Under the provisions of the Act, the Bureau of Education for the Handicapped (BEH) was given four more positions of high administrative level; the National Advisory Committee on Handicapped Children was continued for one more year; funds were authorized for the States to meet "unsatisfied needs" in educating handicapped children under a Federal-State formula; requiring the public schools to place into regular classrooms handicapped children, wherever possible, was also included; and, funds for regional education programs, centers and services, personnel training, research, instructional media and specific learning disabilities were also authorized. The authorization of funds for the whole package for the first fiscal year totalled $631 million.

The turning point was 1974. (See Figure 3.)

4

Public Law 94-142: The Education for All Handicapped Children Act, 1975

S. 6 and H.R. 70: Events of 1974

Because all pending bills in Congress automatically die at the end of the second session of a given Congress, unresolved legislation must be re-introduced in the next Congress as new legislation. Despite the outward appearance of the first session of a new Congress taking a fresh look at such legislation — starting from scratch, as it were — in reality the new Congress is closely tied to recent history. Every time a Committee of the Senate or House holds a hearing on anything, the hearing becomes part of the legislative history of that Committee even if it does not result in an immediate Act of Congress. The link between Congresses depends on something like the following. Only one-third of the Senate seats are up every two years. Few of those running for re-election to the Senate are defeated in the general election (to be sure, Senators retire, are defeated in primaries occasionally, and at times are overwhelmed in the general election). Therefore an investigation by a Senate Committee or Subcommittee in the Second Session of the 93rd Congress in 1974 on a substantive issue — for example, education for the handicapped

72

— will not only be part of recent legislative history, but it will also have been pretty much the work of the same Senators and staff, who are now part of the First Session of the 94th Congress in 1975. Furthermore, although the terms of House members are up at the end of each Congress, generally speaking the leadership of the committees and subcommittees is fairly stable, even after elections resulting in large numbers of "freshmen" coming into the House. The reason is simple enough. The odds are that the leaders come from what are generally considered safe districts, and more than likely they will be back (if they are running for re-election) in the same position of political power in the First Session of the new Congress. Hence the record on education for the handicapped legislation that the 93rd Congress left at the end of 1974 was the underpinning for the 94th Congress in 1975.

That record was made in 1974 by the two subcommittees which dealt with educating handicapped children. The House Subcommittee on Select Education, under the chairmanship of John Brademas, focussed its attention on "new" legislation for education for the handicapped in March, 1974, using Brademas' H.R. 70, *Financial Assistance for Improved Education Services for Handicapped Children*. Senator Harrison Williams, chairman of the Senate Labor and Public Welfare Committee, had introduced his own S. 6, *Education for All Handicapped Children Act*, in the Senate in early 1973. We have briefly analyzed S. 6 previously. Suffice to recall here that Jennings Randolph's Subcommittee on the Handicapped used S. 6 to some extent when it held hearings on S. 896. Eventually S. 896 became part of Public Law 93–380 in 1974. But Randolph's subcommittee also held *another* set of hearings on S. 6 in 1973 and 1974, some of which were outside of Washington. The purpose of these hearings was to broaden the work of the Subcommittee to encourage *more* support not only of interest groups for the handicapped but also state and local agencies. They in turn could use the hearings as platforms for generating more publicity for their points of view. Thus, even though S. 6 did not come to legislative fruition in 1974 as an Act of Congress, the work of the Senate Subcommittee on the Handicapped was the basis for the Senate's approval of Public Law 94-142 in 1975. Hence, another lesson for the student of legislative politics; not only can one Act of Congress lead to another which expands on the substance of the first, but the legislative investigations conducted in previous Congresses can and often do lead to an Act of Congress later on.

The federal role in educating handicapped children was not a dominant one in 1974 despite PL 91-230 and what would lead to PL 93-380 in August of that year. The dollar amount of federal funds actually granted the states for educating the handicapped and for the various projects authorized by the Bureau of Education for the Handicapped was not high. The proportion of federal to state expenditures in the area of handicapped hardly made a serious dent. The federal role seemed to be a "hybrid mixture" of the various roles with the "primary emphasis on innovation and stimulation."[1] The federal government was more of a catalyst than a working partner. Although the states could not really afford full services for handicapped children, they were still reluctant to accept stringent federal rules which were bound to come with every increase in federal funds. The states have always been wary of federal encroachment on what they believe to be essentially state prerogatives. In the area of education for handicapped children, however, the federal government in 1974 was neither encroaching on the states nor fully centralizing its own efforts on behalf of handicapped children. The Department of Health, Education and Welfare had authorized a study of handicapped legislation by the

---

[1] Rand Report, on behalf of the Department of Health, Education and Welfare, quoted in *Hearings, Financial Assistance for Improved Educational Services for Handicapped Children*, H.R. 70, House Subcommittee on Select Education, 93rd Congress, 2nd session, 1974, p. 10.

Rand Corporation which had concluded that the "federal program for aid in educating handicapped had not grown within the framework of a comprehensive plan," but rather was a patchwork of "loosely related activities." The Rand report went on to state that the BEH actually controlled only 54 per cent of the funds the federal government had identified for special education for the handicapped, the rest being in other parts of the government for "vocational, headstart and economically disadvantaged who happened to be handicapped too."[2] As the Senate and House Subcommittees wrestled with S. 6 and H.R. 70, the interest groups for the handicapped and the state and local agencies were very much aware they stood on the threshhold of comprehensive federal legislation.

The House Subcommittee on Select Education and H.R. 70, 1974.

Brademas' Subcommittee on Select Education held hearings on his H.R. 70 on March 6, 7, 18 and 24, 1974. Generally equivalent to the Senate bill, S. 6, introduced by Harrison Williams in the "other body," H.R. 70 was a comprehensive plan which attempted to cement the states to the federal government through certain requirements with which the states had to comply as a condition of receiving federal funds.

If, indeed, the U.S. Commissioner of Education felt that a state was not really expending every effort to provide special educational services for handicapped children or if a state did not adhere to the requirements, the Commissioner of Education could cut off the state from further federal funds. Section 7 of H.R. 70 required the following. To receive federal funds, the state had to:

1. have a comprehensive plan of its own;

[2] *Ibid.*

2. set forth satisfactory assurances that the state's policies and procedures would provide for the services;
3. provide for the identification of all handicapped children in the state;
4. have a plan for institutionalizing those handicapped children who could be trained outside institutions and to provide the procedures for assuring the training and services within the institution;
5. have a system for deinstitutionalizing those handicapped children who could now benefit from "mainstreaming;"
6. provide for due process for the child and the parents to determine the classification of the handicapped;
7. have a plan to train and educate handicapped children who are not part of the public school system and who are not institutionalized;
8. provide procedures for evaluating the plans;
9. provide assurances that the state's records were being kept accurately;
10. provide for a re-evaluation of the state plan, as need be;
11. provide a State Advisory Committee on Education for All Handicapped Children to assist the states in the process;
12. provide a satisfactory method for disbursement of funds to local educational agencies.

Testimony on H.R. 70 included not only that of interest groups but also the views of the new arrivals on the scene, state, and local educational agencies, seventeen of which had state public officials testify or put their opinions on record. Four federal agency officers and a total of 22 other witnesses (not counting several members of Congress) appeared before the Brademas Subcommittee which was trying to bridge the gap between the federal and state governments with a "comprehensive plan" for educating the nation's handicapped children.

Massachusetts and New York can serve as examples of the position of "enlightened" states which were trying to cope with the problems of educating their handicapped children. Francis W. Sargent, Governor of Massachusetts, testified that his state, which had a state program of its own far more advanced than those of most states, needed more federal funds. In fact, the general outline of both H.R. 70 and S. 6 pretty much followed what Massachusetts was doing anyway with its own state legislation. But 50,000 handicapped children enrolled in Massachusetts schools were not receiving any special education and 3,000 were in state institutions "stagnating for lack of care." Massachusetts spent about $100 million annually for education of its handicapped children, $40 million coming from local property taxes, $40 million from the state, and another $20 or so million from the state but earmarked for special education of handicapped children in private schools both in and outside of the State of Massachusetts. Just as Massachusetts was trying to do its job by passing responsibility for educating handicapped children to the local communities with the aid of state funds, so too should the federal government thrust responsibility onto the state and provide federal funds. As a result, federal funds, too, would be passed through to the local communities.[3]

Ewald B. Nyquist, Education Commissioner of the State of New York, welcomed the aims of H.R. 70, testifying that New York had about 459,000 handicapped children, roughly 10 per cent of the total school population, but 200,000 of them received no services whatever. Even a relatively wealthy state like New York could not afford full funding. And, since New York believed in the concept of "mainstreaming" or placing handicapped children in the public schools, it needed

[3] *Ibid.*, p. 51.

more federal funds for training teachers to handle such children.[4]

In general, all state and local officials who testified sent one message — the states would do the job, but they needed huge allocations of federal funds (including money for administering programs for the handicapped).

Patricia Wald, representing the Mental Health Law Project of Washington, D.C., pointed out some telling facts. No matter what the courts said (as in *Mills* and *P.A.R.C.*) or what legislatures say, no matter how good the intentions, "if money is not there, it cannot be allocated." Furthermore, when special education funds "have to compete with regular education funds" at the state level, there is continual war in the state. H.R. 70, therefore, would go a long way to force state responsibility to handicapped children.[5]

A sympathetic House Subcommittee heard friendly testimony from everyone, but the representative of the Nixon Administration, Charles M. Cooke, Jr., Deputy Assistant Secretary for Education Legislation in HEW, testified that if all federal funds allocated for handicapped children (for example, through vocational training, Headstart programs, special institutions like Gallaudet College for the Deaf) were put together it would be found that they totalled about 12 per cent of the $2.4 billion that the states and localities spent for handicapped children in fiscal 1974.[6] Opposing H.R. 70, the Nixon Administration believed that the provisions of the bill would result in a "massive shift toward federal financial and administrative involvement in education for handicapped children" with far-reaching implications upsetting the "heretofore complementary roles of federal, state and local governments." Such a shift was "extremely unwise and unnecessary."[7] Edwin W. Martin, Associate Commis-

[4] *Ibid.*, pp. 60-61.
[5] *Ibid.*, pp. 189-191.
[6] *Ibid.*, pp. 292-293.
[7] *Ibid.*, p. 293.

sioner for Education and head of the BEH and one of the early architects of legislation for the handicapped, testified on the importance of mainstreaming. Even though, he said, "most of us in the field are extraordinarily interested in trying to see handicapped children educated wherever possible with nonhandicapped children in what we call mainstream or integrated settings. . .the probems are very real. . . ."

> Society at large is not used to handicapped people, has not frequently had close dealings with them because we tended to institutionalize them and limit their access to public transportation and public buildings, and teachers, in general, have not had the experience with handicapped children in their training, nor have principals or supervisors, so they are not terribly well able to set a model for the children of the kinds of attitudes, the kinds of understandings, the kinds of personal comfort, which are very necessary if handicapped children are not going to be set aside or isolated and perhaps rejected in a normal school.[8]

Martin was in reality summarizing the philosophical setting of mainstreaming. Mainstreaming handicapped children is a good thing, for them and for the other children. To do it costs money and requires planning. The Nixon Administration was urging a slow-down. Martin, a member of that Administration, was straddling both sides of the fence. But the Committees of the Congress obviously had a "friend in court."

The Senate Subcommittee on the Handicapped and S. 6, 1973–1974

Senator Harrison Williams' S. 6 (previously outlined on pages 62–63) was the vehicle for Jennings Randolph's Senate Subcommittee on the Handicapped hearings in 1973

[8] *Ibid.*, p. 3.

and 1974. Five of the hearings took place in key cities outside Washington (on April 9, 1973 in Newark, N.J., Williams' home state; on May 7, 1973 in Boston, Mass., Senator Kennedy's home state; on May 14, 1973 in Columbia, S.C.; on October 19, 1973 in St. Paul, Minn., Mondale's home state; and, on March 18, 1974 in Harrisburg, Pa., the state in which the *P.A.R.C.* decision had had its original impact and Senator Richard Schweiker's home state.)

S. 6 not only made the emphatic point that a state had to give the federal government assurance that it had a state policy assuring "all handicapped children the right to a free appropriate public education" in order to get federal funds, but also it would have authorized a federal contribution of 75 per cent of the excess costs to educate handicapped children. S. 6, then, was a broader bill than H.R. 70, and the Senate Subcommittee on the Handicapped wrote the stronger record during its hearings.

In the regional hearings, the subcommittee heard testimony from state and local educational agencies, state branches of national interest groups for the handicapped, a number of parents of handicapped children, as well as Senators, Congressmen, state legislators, and state executives. Too, in the regional hearings, the subcommittee was represented not by the full subcommittee, but only one member. For example, in Newark, Senator Williams himself presided along with four professional staff members; in Boston, Williams again with one staff change; in Columbia, Williams and two staffers; in St. Paul, Senator Mondale of Minnesota chaired the hearing, again attended by four staffers; and, in Harrisburg, Pennsylvania Senator Richard Schweiker, a Republican, chaired the hearing along with three staffers. The point is well taken. Without the expertise of the staff, there would be no hearing, no bill, no laws. The regional hearings exposed specific members of the Subcommittee on the Handicapped in their home states and helped cement the relationship between Senators, staff and witnesses. For example, the end of the hearing in Newark, New Jersey was as follows:

SENATOR WILLIAMS: . . . . We have the great advantage of having Mrs. Forsythe on the staff here. How long have you known or been able to communicate with signs, Pat?

MRS. FORSYTHE: 28 years.

SENATOR WILLIAMS: And this was because of your family situation?

MRS. FORSYTHE: Yes, I have a deaf son.

DR. HARRINGTON (a witness): On the other end of the spectrum, Senator, I'm the child of deaf parents.

SENATOR WILLIAMS: I see, Well now, let's just conclude here appropriately. Would you, in signs, thank our friends for the committee?

[Mrs. Forsythe complies in sign language.]

SENATOR WILLIAMS (in jocular fashion): I didn't expect a speech.

[Further compliance by Mrs. Forsythe in sign language, with responding sign language by members of the panel.][9]

The Senate Subcommittee on the Handicapped took testimony from parents and lobbyists of interest groups for the handicapped who pointed out that local educational agencies often "copped out" when it came to actual delivery of compensatory educational services for handicapped children. The witnesses (including an occasional State educational officer) put it in straightforward terms. Federal enforcement is necessary because local educational agencies simply would not carry out their responsibilities on the grounds that they did not have enough money or personnel to do the job. In a sense, therefore, the concept of "pass-

[9] *Hearings, S. 6. Education for All Handicapped Children,* Senate Subcommittee on The Handicapped, First and Second Sessions, 93rd Congress, Part 1, 1973, p. 90.

through" was suspect because passing federal funds through the state directly to local agencies, without strict federal rules including federal oversight, would lead to waste and misallocation of funds at the local level. The subcommittee staff had put together statistics that showed the total cost in excess dollars to serve the 2.85 million handicapped children, *then being served*, would be $2.28 billion. Williams' S. 6 proposed that the federal government supply $1.71 billion (75 per cent) of that to the states.[10] Unless the states followed federal requirements, without the freedom of *unrestricted* "pass-throughs," federal money would disappear (or be "laundered") in local school budgets.

In June, 1974 the Senate Subcommittee on the Handicapped resumed its hearings on S. 6 in Washington. Senator Jennings Randolph pointed out that at the time there were 36 court cases in 24 states that bore on the right to education for handicapped children and 38 court cases in 25 states on the right of handicapped children to due process of law in determining the scope of the states' constitutional responsibilities.[11] Statements supporting S. 6 now rolled in not only from advocacy groups for the handicapped but also other pressure groups like the American Federation of Teachers (AFT of the AFL-CIO), The National Education Association (NEA), the Council of Chief State School Officers, and the National Governors' Conference. A full complement of members of the Senate subcommittee and its staff absorbed the testimony and accepted the basic supposition — more federal involvement was needed.

But the Nixon Administration still balked. Frank S. Carlucci, Under Secretary of HEW, denied that S. 6 was a proper remedy. "The problems of educating handicapped people are more complex," he stated, "than the proposed

[10] *Ibid.*, p. 652.
[11] *Ibid.*, p. 1766.

solution — a massive infusion of funds — contained in S. 6."[12] Carlucci was concerned that S. 6 made no clear distinction between children with major and minor handicaps, underestimated the difficulty in identifying *all* handicapped children, and provided unnecessary funds for states that could well afford the incremental cost of educating their handicapped.[13] The Senate subcommittee paid little heed to the administration, however. Nixon's political strength was at ground zero by then and in less than two months he would be the first President of the United States to resign the office. The Senate subcommittee closed its hearings and made ready for the first session of the new 94th Congress.

The Congressional elections of 1974 did not change the composition of the Senate Subcommittee on the Handicapped since Alan Cranston (Dem. California) and Richard Schweiker (Rep. Pennsylvania), the only two Senators on the subcommittee up for re-election, won handily.

Five freshmen Democrats were placed on the House Subcommittee on Select Education, from the states of Wisconsin, Rhode Island, New York, California and Illinois. Ella Grasso had left the House to become Governor of Connecticut, and Congressmen Mazzoli of Kentucky and Badillo of New York had left the subcommittee although they had been re-elected to the House. The two extra Democrats on the subcommittee brought the total to 10. There was a large turnover on the Republican side with only Peyser returning to the Subcommittee. Three vacancies were filled by veteran Bell of California and newcomers Pressler of South Dakota and Jeffords of Vermont. Despite personnel changes on the House side, the subcommittee remained committed to education for the handicapped. 1975 would be the year for independence of interest groups advocating education for handicapped children.

[12] *Ibid.*, p. 1771.
[13] *Ibid.*, pp. 1771–1775.

THE INTEREST GROUPS KEEP THE
PRESSURE ON — 1975

We have seen that from 1966 to 1974, the handicapped made great strides in removing the barriers to full participation in the educational programs to which they were entitled. They had developed organizationally from scattered awareness and support groups into a formidable political force and, through public education programs, had succeeded in creating a large base of support for programs which would tap the vast potential of the handicapped community. This support was demonstrated through congressional initiatives providing educational programs for handicapped children. The rights issue had been tested time and time again in the courts and the rulings in every case held that children with such special needs were *entitled* to receive educational services at no cost to their parents. By 1974 and the passage of P.L. 93-380, the handicapped had in place at the Federal level:

1. a basic aid to the states program for the education of handicapped children with greatly expanded authority and appropriations;
2. a Bureau of Education for the Handicapped, with top level administrators who served as advocates for handicapped children;
3. set-asides for handicapped children in: vocational education, Title I of ESEA for children in state operated facilities, educational innovation, and Headstart, thus encouraging "mainstreaming" by requiring education officials other than those trained in special education to become involved in programs for the handicapped;
4. model programs for preschoolers and children with specific learning disabilities;
5. a manpower development program;
6. centers for the deaf-blind;

7. innovation, program development and information dissemination projects; and,
8. special media services.

P.L. 93–380, moreover, represented a great step forward in the type and scope of the Federal involvement by facing the "right to education" issue on legislative front. It directed that:

1. states submit comprehensive plans for providing full educational services to handicapped children and a timetable for implementing that goal;
2. EHA funds be used first to provide services for children not enrolled in any educational programs;
3. states prepare a plan for providing due process to all handicapped children served and their parents;
4. states prepare a plan directing efforts to educate children in the "least restrictive environment";
5. states prepare a plan showing how classification procedures will be made culturally and racially unbiased; and,
6. incentive grants be provided to states for the deinstitutionalization of children in state-operated facilities which receive funds under Title I, ESEA.

The handicapped groups had built an impressive record thus far and were encouraged. Their purpose, however, was to represent their constituency on all levels in order to ensure that they received the rights to which they are entitled. Issues of civil rights, however, are never resolved nor the affected group satisfied until those rights are guaranteed, enforced, and demonstrated through full participation in programs. The only passing grade on a civil rights scorecard is 100 per cent.

Although the number of handicapped children receiving an appropriate public education had increased, by early

1975, only about 50 per cent were receiving educational services. This was unacceptable to the interest groups which believed that there was no excuse for the denial of rights. They were supported in this stance by the courts. The opinion of Judge Joseph Waddy in the 1972 *Mills* case stated that:

> The defendants are required by the Constitution of the United States, the District of Columbia Code, and their own regulations to provide a publicly-supported education for these "exceptional" children. Their failure to fulfill this clear duty to include and retain these children in the public school system, or otherwise provide them with publicly-supported education, and their failure to afford them due process hearings and periodical review, cannot be excused by the claim that there are insufficient funds. . . . The inadequacies of the District of Columbia Public School System, whether occasioned by insufficient funding or administrative inefficiency, certainly cannot be permitted to bear more heavily on the "exceptional" or handicapped child than on the normal child.

While encouraged by the progress in providing education for the handicapped, the interest groups found that gradual phasing in of services was too slow. While lack of funds, personnel, and an appropriate delivery system were all real problems, the ultimate reality was that "no services" being provided to 50 per cent of the children was in violation of their rights.

The strategy, therefore, was to follow the path of other civil rights legislation by authorizing the establishment of a compliance mechanism which would impose harsh penalties on those states not meeting the mandate of "free appropriate public education." This proposal would go further than the state plan requirements outlined in P.L. 93–380 in two ways:

1. A system of enforcement would be set up at federal

and state levels to monitor continually the provision of the guarantees; and,

2. Strict, and definite penalities would be imposed for failure to comply.[14]

The 94th Congress — Public Law 94–142 is Enacted, 1975

The interest groups representing handicapped children were also concerned that Congress, the Administration, and other State and local education officials were losing sight of the original issue as the 94th Congress began. S6 and H.R. 70 had several differences as would their offspring introduced in the new year. When a bill is introduced, especially one which has such a broad impact on so many different groups, the process of debate and refinement which is necessary to accommodate all these interests often seems to the outsider to be "nit-picking." it is important to go through this process, however, so that opposition to the proposal is minimized; however, the trick is to make everybody happy without undermining the purpose of the bill and losing everything. All this negotiation takes time and deadlocks on certain issues can be formed, in effect killing the bill without substantive reason.

Since this bill directly benefited the constituency represented by the handicapped interest groups, their job was to orchestrate the passage of a clean, clear, comprehensive mandate as smoothly and as quickly as possible.

In January 1975, the outlook for introduction and early passage of new bills directed toward the education of the handicapped was excellent. Discussions about the appropriate federal role in the education of the handicapped had been underway since 1972, and everybody knew that a program was going to be passed in 1975. The advocacy groups were

[14] Letter to Congress from CEC January 10, 1973.

concerned, however, that differences about design of a funding formula, details to be included in the individual education plan and other problems, would burden the progress of a bill guaranteeing participation of handicapped children.

Accordingly, they set to work developing a dialogue with education interests, the Congress and others to preserve the major provisions of the proposals.

Senator Williams reintroduced S. 6 on January 15, 1975. Hearings were held on April 8, 9, and 15, 1975 in Washington, D.C. These three days finished the set of hearings on the legislation which recorded the views of over 100 individuals representing legislators, parents, parent organizations, consumers, education associations, and educators from all levels. S. 6 was ordered reported from the Subcommittee on the Handicapped on May 12. Eight days later, the full Committee on Labor and Public Welfare reported it to the Senate which passed S. 6 on June 18, 1975.

On the House side, no bill was introduced until May 21, 1975. However, hearings were held on April 9 and 10 of that year and drafts of the proposed legislation had been sent to key interest groups. A final hearing was held on the measure, H.R. 7217, at the request of the Ford Administration on June 9, 1975. After a polite nod to the objections of the Administration, the Subcommittee unanimously reported H.R. 7217 with amendments to the full Committee on Education and Labor on June 10, 1975. The measure, as amended, was ordered reported to the House floor on June 17, 1975 and passed The House a month later.

After resolving their differences in a joint conference committee, the bill was passed and sent to the President who signed it on November 29, 1975.

HOUSE VERSION — H.R. 7217

With the impressive hearing record and the mandate in the one year authorization for increased funds, the House subcommittee began to work on drafting its version of the Education for All Handicapped Children Act. S. 6 had been introduced in the Senate and was moving forward at full speed. Both Houses were under pressure to expand the authorization for these programs in time to affect the FY 1976 appropriations bill. Negotiations had been ongoing throughout the first 5 months of the year in hopes of drafting a bill which for the most part would be acceptable to all parties. The Subcommittee on Select Education agreed on a bill May 20th and it was introduced on May 21 as H.R. 7217.

Despite the fact that the education community, those state and local education agencies which would ultimately be providing the services, had supported the expansion of Federal assistance to programs for the education of the handicapped during the 1973, 1974 hearings, what was emerging from the subcommittee in the form of the bill was not totally acceptable to them. The basis for their support early in the discussions and the thrust of a new program included:

1. a philosophical commitment to providing equal educational opportunity for handicapped children, regardless of whether or not the delivery system existed;
2. a firmly imbedded mandate from the courts to provide educational services to handicapped children;
3. the hope of a significant Federal fiscal contribution to programs for the handicapped; and,
4. the expectation that a new Federal program would increase authorizations for funds without significantly changing the requirements of P.L. 93-380. That is, it was believed that the new monies would be channelled through existing state and local governance structures, would help those states with handicapped programs well underway to underwrite their costs, and provide funds to states with little involvement in this area to set up their own programs.

These assumptions were founded on what was previously

thought to be the appropriate Federal role in education in general. The House bill, as introduced, however, contradicted these beliefs and state and local education officials began to have serious reservations about the bill. For one thing, the bill provided grants directly from the U.S. Commissioner of Education to local education agencies. Naturally, the local school districts approved of getting the money directly but shied away from the requirements which were attached especially considering the small federal contribution. They figured that even if the appropriation of $100,000,000 provided in the FY 75 appropriations was doubled, per capita benefits of $40 per child would result. At the time, the average cost of educating the handicapped child exceeded $2,000 per child. Therefore, they supported a local entitlement which would pick up a significant percentage of the excess cost.

States agreed to a small extent with the Administration's (through the Bureau of Education for the Handicapped) position that funds be targeted by states to further their coordination and technical assistance efforts. The small amount of funds, they believed, could only support catalytic efforts to reach the goal of equal education opportunities and should supplement state efforts. The second concern was the change in philosophy from federal support of state administered programs for handicapped education to a federal system of handicapped education as represented by direct grants to local school districts by the U.S. Commissioner of Education. States argued that the approximately 4 per cent federal contribution given to locals outlined very specific requirements about how to run handicapped programs but lacked a method for coordination with state programs which were picking up the remaining 96 per cent. This method would cause confusion and be disruptive of state efforts on behalf of the handicapped. Underneath all this, of course, was the fear on the part of the state and local governments that the result would represent a big step toward federal control of education.

The interest groups for the handicapped preferred state plans and responsibility but agreed that the money should go directly to the local level with strings attached to every dollar. It was reasoned that if the money flowed through fewer bureaucratic levels, more would go directly toward services for children. In addition, the level of competence in special education and the stage of development of such programs in the 50 states varied tremendously. Therefore, they advocated passage of a national standard for educating the handicapped, reasoning that this would force states with no program to get one and that states with good efforts underway would already be in compliance. This reasoning was sound in theory but not in practice.

States had another major concern with the House bill which was also linked to their fear of a federal takeover. H.R. 7217 provided for the establishment of a planning and advisory council appointed by the Governor to make evaluations on the program. They argued that this circumvented states' governance structures and that the federal government could achieve as much accountability through the State Education Agency which was responsible for state programs as well as for state plans.

The interest groups preferred accountability at the state level but not housed in the state program office. They recognized that compliance enforcement at the national level was impractical but wanted to insure that impartiality was preserved.

The local education agencies, preferred compliance monitoring carried out at the national level. While we often think of our federal system as being two tiered, the local governments are an integral part of this system. In education, most local school districts are independent of state systems and control has been achieved by states through the same means as the federal government, through requirements they place on their funds. The position, therefore, was clearly taken early in the game. The states wanted money given to them in accordance with a state plan which outlined how they intended to achieve the full service goal. The locals wanted the money to come directly to them with little supervision by the states. At the federal level, the Administration really did not want any part of it, while the interest groups for handicapped children wanted everybody involved and checks everywhere.

S.6 — THE SENATE VERSION

Both Houses intended that a comprehensive bill would be passed early in the 94th Congress. By April, 1975, however, there was additional pressure to expand the authorization in time to affect the FY 1976 appropriation bill. The Senate bill provided more funds for the programs and retained the State Education Agencies' authority to distribute funds to locals, subject to the priorities established in the bill. A compliance entity was also established in each state outside of the State Education Agency whose job was to conduct periodic evaluations to determine whether the state and local education agencies were in compliance.

In general, both House and Senate bills provided support for extensive expansion of state services and administration procedures. The bill moved swiftly through both Houses and the conference began in September 1975 to resolve the differences in the two bills. What came out of that conference would shape the course of education for the handicapped in the future so all parties, the education community, the administration and interest groups were active in the resolution of differences.

The Joint Conference — Where it All Comes Together

Until the mid 1970's, conference committee sessions were closed to everyone except the conferees and their staff. Not until December 1976, however, were the House rules revised to require that all meetings be open to the public unless otherwise voted by the full House. During the conference on S.6 in 1975, therefore, the lobbyists, the press and the administration had to do some careful negotiating before and during the conference without actually being present in the sessions. This negotiation was necessary in order to reach a compromise that would ensure passage on the floors of both Houses as well as ensure that the bill would be signed by the President. The conferees have limits on what they can do, however:

1. Conferees may not strike or amend any portion of a bill about which there is no disagreement. In other words, if the language is the same in both versions, then it is not conferenceable.
2. New language may not be added unless it is germane (or relates) to the difference between the two versions.
3. If the disagreement involves dollar amounts, the compromise must fall between the two figures in the bills. For instance, if the Senate version authorizes $100 for a program and the House authorizes $200, the compromise figure must be between $100 and $200. Of course, they usually end up splitting it down the middle.

These ground rules appear to limit the authority of the conferees but actually give them quite a bit of freedom. They bear in mind, however, that the conference report must be agreed upon by both Houses again, and pride of authorship must not be hurt.

By the time the Conference began, all the participants in

the process had done their homework and communicated their preferences to the conferees. The staff had also been active in reviewing these comments and advising on language which would be acceptable to all parties without undermining the interest of the legislation. The conferees met in early September and began sifting through the disagreements. Three major issues emerged in which all the participants had an interest and which illustrates conference procedures.

The first issue involved the formula for allocating funds. Both S.6 and H.R. 7217 provided an entitlement formula that authorized such sums as may be necessary to carry out the provisions of the act and then provided a formula for determining how much money would be needed. The House bill authorized expenditures based on 50 per cent of the national average per pupil cost of education times the number of handicapped children served. The Senate formula based the Federal contribution on $300 times the number of handicapped children served. The House version provided for a permanent authorization, (that is there was no expiration date fixed in the bill) while the Senate version expired on September 30, 1979.

The handicapped interest groups preferred the House version of the formula provisions. They argued that a permanent authorization would provide stability in the legislation so that the program could progress in a consistent manner. In addition, they did not want to open the program up to amendment before it could become fully operational. They also preferred using a percentage factor so that variables such as inflation would not jeopardize program funding in real dollars. They also recommended that the total authorization not be lowered to increase the expectation of full funding.

The Ford Administration's representatives maintained that the bill was unacceptable to them unless major modifications were made. They felt that the multibillion dollar authorization was unrealistic and would create false expectations among the handicapped. They were also concerned that the new formula would increase the likelihood of mislabeling students as handicapped by placing a Federal "bounty" on the heads of children served. Therefore, they recommended a lower authorization.

The education community shared the Administration's fears about the creation of unrealistic expectations. While the larger amount authorized by the House bill was needed by state and local agencies, the reality was that full funding by later appropriations legislation was not likely to be achieved. What they were saying, in fact, was that if the Federal government wanted a program carried out it would have to pay for it. Both bills also specified an effective date for the new formula to "kick in." The interest groups supported the Senate FY 1977 implementation date while the education groups felt that the House version starting the formula in FY 1978 would give state legislatures and education agencies more time to fulfill the requirements for receiving funds.

A second major issue involved the level of government which would receive the funds to serve children: state versus local. The Senate bill allocated funds directly to the State Education Agency, 40 per cent of which would be allocated to local education agencies (LEA's) within the states based on the number of children in need of service. The 60 percent remaining would be used by the State Education Agencies for the priorities outlined in the bill. The House provision provided that the total amount minus a 5 per cent set aside for state administration be passed through to local education agencies based on the number of handicapped children in the districts.

The interest groups urged that the House provision providing funds directly to school districts be accepted by the conferees because the final responsibility for providing services rested with the local education agency. However, they also supported a 20 per cent setaside for state education agencies provided that these funds be used for technical assistance activities; to provide additional funds to districts with high concentrations of unserved handicapped children, to assist districts with higher "startup" costs, to support activities to protect the rights of handicapped children and their parents; to stimulate pre-school development, and to provide support to regional programs. They also supported the House provision which prescribed that several requirements be met by the local school districts before the money could pass through. Two things would be accomplished if this language were accepted. The money would be channeled directly to the agency providing services, and services would be provided in the manner outlined in federal law. The state would have very little discretion in how this allocation was handled and funds could not be distributed on the basis of assurances by the state that programs would be carried out.

The Ford Administration did not support the enactment of S.6 unless major revisions were made during the conference. They argued that the provisions contained in both bills would alter drastically the traditional Federal-State roles in education and that the state plans required under PL 93–380 clearly showed that the states were undertaking in earnest to fulfill the goal of full service to handicapped children.

The local school districts supported receiving the funds directly (the method of directly funding local government is called "pass-through"). They reasoned that the programs carried out in the local school districts by local education agencies should be funded without added restrictions by the state. They argued that they were the appropriate recipients of the funds with only a small setaside for states. They also wanted to be sure that once a school district became dependent upon a program of this size, changes in intra-state allocations could not be accomplished. They were especially concerned about the House provisions allowing the state educational agency to reduce funds from one school district at full services to another district which was not.

The states of course supported the Senate provision providing for only 40 per cent "pass-through" to locals and 60 per cent reserved to the states. They argued that most states required through their own laws that the SEA implement a full education service goal by a specified time period. The 100 per cent "pass-through" provision in the House bill would weaken its ability to implement good statewide programs. In addition, the bills outlined additional services and facilities which should be established and coordinated at the state level. The teacher training and demonstration programs required under the act were obviously state functions and required more funds than the 5 per cent setaside in the House bill. In addition, the due process channels and program evaluations could not be monitored at the local level and yet were an integral part of the process. Lastly, the states wanted to retain flexibility in allocating funds for several reasons. The state ultimately had to guarantee that services were provided to all children. While local districts argued that schools who had full service early should not be penalized, the states believed that they should be able to target funds to areas of the greatest need. Plans for the equalization of school finance were also in full swing in most states and when the funds reached into the multibillion dollar range, state formulas were going to suffer.

Another issue which perhaps was considered the most important issue by the interest groups concerned the establishment of an in-state compliance mechanism. Both the House and Senate versions mandated the establishment of a compliance entity. The House version included the following steps:

1. Each school district had to make available a grievance procedure to investigate and resolve complaints. Resolution of complaints were to be reported to the SEA.
2. SEA could investigate cases and had to hear appeals for review. If the SEA determined that there had been a failure to comply with the act, it could correct such

failures by informal methods and formal methods when necessary.

3. The SEA had to transmit a report of its actions to the U.S. Commissioner of Education.
4. The SEA was to take into account past failures and its determination in considerations of future allotments to the local education agencies.

The Senate version established a compliance entity whose membership would include handicapped persons or parents and others experienced in education of the handicapped at the state level. The responsibilities of this panel included:

1. periodic evaluations of compliance throughout the state.
2. review of complaints and determinations of non-compliance and order of remedies.
3. notification to the U.S. Commissioner of non-compliance.

The interest groups had maintained a position throughout the legislative history that a compliance mechanism was absolutely necessary to "put some teeth" into the law ensuring educational rights of the Handicapped. They saw several essential ingredients for such a mechanism. These included:

1. authority to monitor regularly compliance by state and local school districts.
2. clear linkages to the U.S. Office of Education through required reports of non-compliance.
3. a reasonable degree of independence from the educational system through membership on such panel representing a cross-section of the handicapped community (i.e. parents, educators and advocates.)

The advocacy groups sought to strike a balance of authority between state and local education establishment responsibilities in education and the federal government responsibilities to guarantee constitutional rights. Compromise language was suggested which combined what they believed were the best features of both bills as well as some additional clarification. The elements of this compromise included an assurance of due process in any proceeding involving such a mechanism and an assurance that some form of the "futility doctrine" be available. The "futility doctrine" meant that not all steps of an administrative remedy must necessarily be exhausted prior to consideration in the courts if there is no reasonable hope of satisfaction through this process. In other words, the system they wanted would stipulate that the administrative system was neither an alternative to court action nor did it have to precede court action. Judicial review must be permitted at any stage of the review. In addition, they wanted provision that *federal* district courts would have original jurisdiction for any action arising under the law. They also wanted precise time-lines for results to be obtained in any grievance procedure. Lastly, the advocacy groups wanted to include a penalty for state and local education agencies of loss of federal funds for non-compliance with the federal law.

The education community at the state level was appalled at the elaborate system proposed in the Senate bill and the amplification of this procedure suggested by the advocacy groups. They argued that it was totally inappropriate for the federal government to mandate the creation of a compliance entity outside of the established state and local governance structure. Any procedure for ensuring due process in addition to those mandated by states would be redundant and disruptive and provide an opportunity for adversary relationships to develop. Accordingly, they favored the plan outlined in the House bill.

The Administration opposed the establishment of a new compliance entity as it would assume authority which belonged to state and local education agencies. It argued that rights were already protected by existing administrative and judicial procedures and, therefore, supported the House provisions which used the existing state and local structures.

These issues were the most controversial in the conference and about which representatives of all the affected constituencies were concerned. The position of each group was predictable, however. The interest groups wanted all children served within a specified period of time and wanted the federal government to ensure that this was accomplished. State agencies saw this legislation as an opportunity to get federal funds to achieve their own timetables and fulfill their agenda for serving the handicapped, but not a bill that would drastically alter Federal-State roles in the education process. The local education agencies, most of them with a significant amount of independence in their own districts, wanted to minimize the authority of state education agencies and maximize their own direct contact with the federal government in the area of Federal assistance. Their independence would not be further eroded by the placement of additional state requirements on the federal assistance. The Administration was serious in its opposition to the bill and the threat of a veto was in the air. President Ford believed that the role of the federal government as outlined in S.6 was inappropriate, that the fiscal requirements of the act were unrealistic, and the new procedures for special education were not only an unwelcome federal intrusion but also an expensive program to implement.

The Major Compromises and Passage of P.L. 94-142

The bill as reported from conference resolved the three major issues in compromises designed to satisfy to a certain extent *all* of the different interests.

The conference substitute provided for a permanent authorization to take effect October 1, 1977. The maximum amount of a grant entitled to each state would be equal to the average number of handicapped children aged 3–21 who were receiving special education and related services on October 1 and February 1 of the preceding fiscal year times a percentage of the national average per pupil expenditure for the nation. The percentage of the federal contribution was set at 5 per cent for FY 78, 10 per cent for FY 1979; 20 per cent for FY 80; 30 per cent for FY 81; and 40 per cent for each fiscal year thereafter. No state was to receive less than it received in the preceding fiscal year. In addition, no state was to have a count that exceeded 12 per cent of its total population aged 5–17.

The compromise softened some of the objections of the participants. A permanent authorization provided stability and demonstrated a federal commitment to the handicapped; the gradually increasing authorization based on a percentage of the average per pupil expenditure rather than a fixed sum ensured a hedge against inflation but softened the blow of a multi-billion dollar authorization in the first year, allowing BEH to make budget requests in manageable increments. The 12 per cent limitation as the number of children to be counted lessened the fear that children would be mislabeled in order to get the "bounty" provided by the Federal government.

The distribution of funds to state and local agencies was resolved as follows: Beginning in FY 1978, 25 per cent of the funds received by a state could be used by the state in a manner consistent with the priorities outlined in the law and the remaining 75 per cent was to be passed through to the local education agencies, according to the ratio of the number of handicapped children served among all the LEA's in the state. In addition, each state was permitted to spend a small percentage of federal funds for administration.

This second compromise helped satisfy the local agencies by guaranteeing them a significant percentage of the funds, the state agencies by allowing them some funds to carry out the duties other than administrative required in the Act, and the interest groups which wanted most of the money to go where the children were being served while providing that the states would have reasonable federal assistance above administration for ensuring that services were delivered at the local level.

The third major compromise involved the compliance entity. The conferees accepted the House provisions with certain conforming amendments on review and due process procedures. Compliance review and grievance procedures were to be within the state governance structure. The State Education Agency was to be the first appeal body and would make determinations of failure by the Local Education Agency. Certain due process procedures were reaffirmed such as the right to counsel at hearings, the provision of transcripts or recordings in the parents' native language and the right to a hearing by an impartial hearing officer. In addition, actions could be brought in the U.S. district courts to appeal the determination of the SEA.

This compromise helped resolve the Administration's question of the appropriate federal role and answered in part the objections of the states about interference in their state governance structures. At the same time, the interest groups' concerns about impartial due process procedures and recourse to U.S. courts were addressed. Enough checks and balances were built into the system to ensure compliance.

Other agreements had been reached throughout the conference, and the compromises made satisfied each constituency enough to ensure the passage of the bill and fend off a Ford veto. The bill quickly eased through the Senate and the House, as is usually the case with bills that emerge from a joint conference, and became Public Law 94-142 when President Ford signed it into law on November 29, 1975.

The process was by no means over, however, and each party held reservations about the law. The interest groups for the handicapped now had a comprehensive education act, which was permanently authorized and would not automatically have to be subject to further extensions. The way seemed clearer toward providing every handicapped child with a free appropriate public education. If the states accepted federal money, they would have to comply with federal regulations. The local educational agencies would have more money to work with. But there were still problems. How would the Bureau of Education for the Handicapped write the regulations to carry out the intent of P.L. 94-142? How could an accurate count of identifiable handicapped children be done in the first place? Was there enough money to do the job? Would federal regulations really keep the states and local educational agencies from wasting federal money? Would, in fact, handicapped children get an education appropriate to their needs and would they be educated to the fullest extent possible? Would they be mainstreamed properly — and would it work?

These and other questions had to be dealt with on the other side of the legislative process, that of the enforcement of the Act of Congress by the federal agency having jurisdiction. Here too the interest groups would have an impact. A regulatory remedy, now that the legislative remedy seemed resolved, would now have to take shape.

5

The Implementation
of PL 94-142, 1976-1977

"Rounding Off the Edges:" Writing the Regulations

A "free appropriate public education" for handicapped children took a significant step towards reality when President Gerald R. Ford somewhat reluctantly signed S. 6 into law on November 29, 1975. Ford feared that PL 94-142 would raise the hopes of handicapped children and their families to an unrealistic level. He was pessimistic about the federal government's ability to match Congress' great expectations with the appropriations necessary to meet the high costs of providing services and education to the nation's handicapped children. PL 94-142, too, was a federal "carrot," enticing the states with federal funds that might prove too big for the states to swallow or not savory enough to be worth their partaking. An adherent of the Republican party philosophy that the states should not be unduly regulated by Washington, Ford also saw further encroachment on them by the federal bureaucracy engaging in detailed regulation over state and local education agencies. But a veto of the bill would bring down on him the wrath of the interest groups for the handicapped. They had not labored long and hard for this comprehensive federal commitment to take such a veto lightly, and the Congress was by then thoroughly committed to their cause. The President, therefore, signed the measure into law but not without expressing his doubts about its efficacy.

The intent of PL 94–142 was to provide federal funds for helping the states to educate their handicapped children. The states did not have to accept federal funds, of course, but if they did so, they would be compelled to fulfill all aspects of PL 94–142. Once a state agreed to accept such funds and the Bureau of Education for the Handicapped approved the state plan, the state was then obligated to guarantee its handicapped children a free appropriate public education without cost to them or their families. Unquestionably, PL 94–142 was ambitious.

The Major Features of PL 94–142

THE FORMULA

The formula for determining the federal contribution to the states was based on an increasing percentage of the National Average Per Pupil Expenditure (NAPPE) multiplied by the number of handicapped children being served by the state. The percentage of NAPPE authorized by PL 94–142 started with 5 per cent in 1978 and went to 40 per cent of NAPPE for fiscal year 1982 and beyond, in increasing steps (10 per cent in 1979, 20 per cent in 1980 and 30 per cent in 1981).

EXCESS COSTS

Congress was careful to write into the law that federal funds were not to be comingled with state and local educational funds or used to supplant them. The federal contribution was to be used only for costs *in excess* of costs for educating children in the regular school program. School districts, therefore, could only apply for federal assistance for educational costs incurred *above* the average per pupil expenditures for all children in the districts.

"PASS-THROUGH"

"Pass-through" funds occur when federal funds are allocated to local government agencies "through the state" by federal law. The state has no direct control over such "pass-through" funds and is simply the funnel for their distribution. PL 94-142 allowed state education agencies to retain 50 per cent of the total state allocation and the remaining 50 per cent was to be "passed through" to the local education agencies. By fiscal year 1980 (which began on October 1, 1979) "pass-through" funds were to increase to 75 per cent of the federal contribution of monies allocated to each state.

PRIORITIES

The priorities for receiving services were broadened under PL 94-142 over those mandated in PL 93-380. First priority children included the unserved and second priority children included the severely handicapped within each disability receiving inadequate services.

INDIVIDUALIZED EDUCATION PROGRAM (IEP)

PL 94-142 mandates that each handicapped child must have an individualized education program which sets out in writing what special education and related services will actually be provided to the child. The IEP is to be developed by the local education agency (or representative of the agency), the teacher(s), the parents or guardian and, where appropriate, the child.

THE APPROPRIATE ENVIRONMENT

In order for states to be eligible for participation in the benefits of PL 94-142, they must establish procedures "to assure that to the maximum extent appropriate, handicapped children, including children in public or private institutions or other care facilities, are educated with children who are not handicapped, and that special classes, separate schooling, or other removal of handicapped children from the regular educational environment occurs only when the nature or severity of the handicap is such that education in regular classes with the use of supplementary aids and services cannot be achieved satisfactorily. . ." This provision became known as the requirement to "mainstream" and would emerge in time as a major issue, although under the euphemism — "the least restrictive environment."

STATE EDUCATION AGENCY RESPONSIBILITY

The State Education Agency in each state was deemed responsible for insuring that all the requirements of PL 94-142 were being carried out and that all education programs within the state for handicapped children met standards set by the agency.

Other Requirements for Both States and Local School Districts

1. They had to establish procedures to identify their handicapped children. For purposes of counting such

children, each child could be counted only once, even though some had more than one handicap.

2. They had to establish a timetable for meeting the "full service goal" established by PL 94-142.

3. When establishing the Individualized Education Program, the local school district Board of Education and the State had to guarantee due process procedures to ensure fairness to the handicapped child.

4. Parent or guardian consultation with the school had to be on a regular basis.

5. Tests and evaluations had to be non-discriminatory.

In the event that the state or local school district failed to comply with the various provisions of PL 94-142, the federal government has the right to withdraw federal funds authorized under PL 94-142 as well as federal funds authorized under other Acts of Congress indirectly related to the education of the handicapped (Part H of Title I of the Elementary and Secondary Education Act, Title III of the same Act, and the Vocational Education Act).

Public Law 94-142 was now in place. But once a bill becomes a law, it becomes the responsibility of the executive branch to implement its provisions. Questions about how the intent of the Congress is to be achieved in practice, within the provisions and context of the public law, are answered by the federal administering agency through the development of regulations, or as they are commonly known, the "regs." The process by which the "regs" are written is lengthy and represents another opportunity for the various actors — the interest groups, the Congress and the staff, the states etc., — to resolve their concerns about a program. Some would say that regulations are even more important than the Act of Congress itself because they govern the day-to-day operations of an idea that has been written into a statute. Before we go into the implementation of PL 94-142 and the writing of the "regs" which would govern the administering of the Education for All Handicapped Children Act, we must first examine and explain the development of another important federal role in the lives of handicapped persons, not just children of school age, Section 504 of the Rehabilitation Act of 1973, (PL 93-112). (See Figure 4.)

Section 504 of the Rehabilitation Act of 1973 (PL 93-112)

We have been dealing with but one part of the problems of the handicapped, that of educating and servicing handicapped children. PL 94-142 was not the only Congressional response to the difficulties facing handicapped persons in the conduct of their daily lives. In late September, 1973, the 93rd Congress passed, over President Ford's veto, PL 93-112, the vocational Rehabilitation Act of 1973. A key section of PL 93-112 is Section 504 which states:

> No otherwise qualified handicapped individual in the United States, as defined in Section 7(6), shall, solely by reason of his handicap, be excluded from the participation in, be denied the benefits of, or be subjected to discrimination *under any program or activity receiving Federal financial assistance.* (Italics added.)

Obviously, the federal regulations enforcing Section 504 could be another important component for guaranteeing the right of handicapped children to a free appropriate public education, although in 1973 PL 94-142 was yet in the offing. The Office of Civil Rights of the Department of Health, Education and Welfare was charged with the responsibility for implementing Section 504 of the Rehabilitation Act. HEW delayed publishing federal regulations for the carrying out of Section 504's provisions, and in October, 1974 the Senate Committee on Labor and Public Welfare took note of the fact that 504 regulations had not been put into effect even

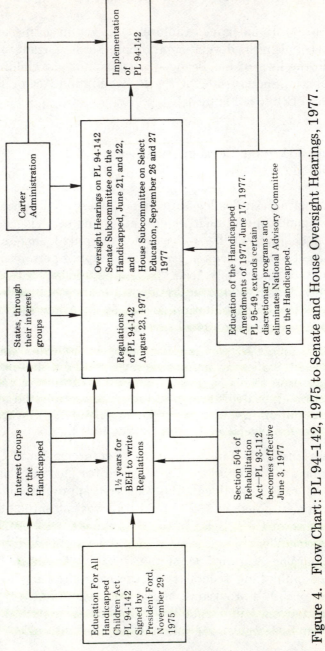

Figure 4. Flow Chart: PL 94-142, 1975 to Senate and House Oversight Hearings, 1977.

though the Rehabilitation Act was one year old.[1] In November, 1975, PL 94-142 was enacted by Congress. Now the regulations for these two mandates — Section 504 and PL 94-142 — were in the process of being drafted at the same time. Every effort was made by the Bureau of Education for the Handicapped to cooperate with HEW's Office of Civil Rights, which would be charged with enforcing Section 504. In a certain sense, the two mandates paralleled each other. Section 504 was a civil rights statute — the stick — while PL 94-142 was a program mandate — the carrot. They both contained provisions for the potential withdrawal of federal funds from the states for noncompliance. These two approaches to enforcement of "rights" of handicapped persons were a "requirement" that they not be discriminated against. They permitted withdrawal of federal funds by HEW in the event that HEW's Office of Civil Rights (OCR) or Bureau of Education for the Handicapped (BEH) found that discrimination did indeed continue to exist. The right of handicapped *children*, who were encompassed in Section 504's handicapped *persons*, to an education on a nondiscriminatory basis became thus even more firmly rooted. With passage of PL 94-142 in November, 1975, the BEH then had to write and implement federal regulations pertaining to both Section 504 and PL 94-142. Every effort was now made by BEH to cooperate with HEW's OCR. For one thing, if the regulations implementing Section 504, a civil rights statute, paralleled the rules for PL 94-142, a program statute, State and local agencies would be more willing to comply with the Education for All Handicapped Children Act. In other words, if a "free appropriate public education" is a civil right under Section 504, which does not provide for federal financial assistance, then local school districts might as well use PL 94-142 federal funds to provide that education. Cooperation seemed to be a very logical method,

[1]*Amicus.*, Vol. 2, No. 5, September 1977, 34-35.

especially since BEH thought the 504 regulations would be issued well in advance of their deadline for PL 94-142. Several problems got in the way however. Because of the brevity of Section 504, its potentially enormous impact on the society, and the lack of legislative history (it had whipped through the Congress very quickly), it took a long time for OCR to come up with some reasonable standards to implement it. As a matter of fact, it took two years and eight months for any public action to be taken. On April 28, 1976 President Ford ordered HEW "to coordinate the implementation of Section 504. . .by all Federal Departments and agencies. . .so that consistent policies, practices, and procedures were adopted with respect to enforcement of Section 504."[2] On May 17, 1976, HEW issued a Notice of Intent (NOI) to Issue Proposed Rules which raised several questions and issues for comment. Based on public comments, the Notice of Proposed Rulemaking (NPRM) was published in the *Federal Register* on July 16, 1976. More then 700 comments were received by HEW in response to these rules and input also was received at twenty-two public meetings held around the country. Final rules were placed on the then Secretary of HEW David Mathews' desk late that fall for his signature. Mathews was unwilling to sign the final regulations, however, and a district judge ordered that he promulgate the regulations. Mathews felt that since a new Administration was coming into office in January, 1977, following the election of Jimmy Carter in November 1976, he should not put the Section 504 regulations into effect. The Federal District Court felt otherwise, but the U.S. Court of Appeals permitted Mathews to delay the signing until after January 20, 1977, the date of Carter's inauguration as President.[3] Carter's HEW Secretary, Joseph Califano, now had to learn as much

---

[2] *Ibid.* See also *Federal Register*, April 29, 1976.

[3] *Cherry et al., v. Mathews, et al.* 419 F. Supp. 922 (D.D.C. 1976). See also *Amicus*, Vol. 2, No. 2, February, 1977, 27-28.

as he could about the complexities of HEW as quickly as possible. He did not embrace the final regulations on Section 504 as soon as taking office, thus earning the enmity of the organizations for handicapped persons. He announced that he would appoint a Task Force within the Department to review the rules once more and talk to groups for the handicapped and other interested parties, including employers, education representatives, state and local governments and so forth. By the spring of 1977, the handicapped population was furious and a number of handicapped persons occupied Califano's offices at HEW in Washington in April, 1977, demanding that he sign the "regs" and thereby set in motion the procedures for their obtaining their legal rights under the Rehabilitation Act (PL 93-112). On April 28, 1977 Califano gave in and signed the "regs" which went into effect June 3, 1977.[4]

PL 94-142 had become law in late November, 1975. The federal regulations implementing that law did not go into effect until August 23, 1977, a little more than two and a half months after Section 504's regulations became operative. HEW (through OCR and BEH) was of course considering the "regs" for both laws (PL 93-112's Section 504 and PL 94-142) during the same relative time. The regulations were thus coordinated. In the final rules and regulations for PL 94-142, for example, Section 504 of PL 93-112 is made reference to in several instances. The BEH took the opportunity, in the "regs" for PL 94-142, to point out that even if a local agency refused PL 94-142 federal funds, it would still have to comply with Section 504, which had no program funds. A local school district, then, might just as well take the federal funds from PL 94-142 with all the "strings" that went with it as not. Because the "regs" of PL 94-142 affected handicapped *children* and their education more directly than those of Section 504 — although making a clear

---

[4] *Amicus, ibid.,* see also *Federal Register*, May 4, 1977.

distinction between the "civil rights" requirement of both would be difficult — we shall now pay more detailed attention to their promulgation.

Implementing PL 94-142 — The Bureau of Education for the Handicapped

The Education for All Handicapped Children Act was a very detailed piece of legislation in terms of not only establishing broad policy guidelines but also outlining procedures for accomplishing these national goals. The staffs of the House Subcommittee on Select Education and Senate Subcommittee on the Handicapped had written as much restrictive language within the law as they felt they could get away with. Several gray areas remained, however, and the law was turned over to the Department of Health, Education and Welfare's Office of Education for implementation through regulations. The law stipulated that the "regs" must be issued no later than one year from enactment. Public participation in the regulation development process for PL 94-142 was unprecedented. The Bureau of Education for the Handicapped, which was charged finally with administering the law, decided to open up the process at the beginning because of the great public interest in this issue. Before this time, the drafting of rules for legislated programs was done "in-house" with very little opportunity for input from organizations or individuals having a stake in the result. Usually, a task force was formed within the agency responsible for the program and comments were requested only *after* proposed rules had been drafted. Decisions, such as what issues would be addressed in the regulations, were made well in advance of this announcement and, therefore, most people perceived their own impact on the regulations to be minimal.

Since 1976, however, regulations policy has been drastically revised to include formal procedures for public involvement. In a memorandum from HEW Secretary David Mathews, procedures were established for HEW which included an additional step in the rulemaking process. A Notice of Intent (NOI) to issue regulations was required. This "mechanism". . .was to be. . .liberally used to permit interested outside groups and other members of the public to have an impact on the decision-making process at an early stage. In addition, ". . .other channels of communication with the public will be liberally used in order to reach as many interested individuals and organizations as possible. . ." Moreover, public hearings were required and "in the spirit of openness, a draft regulation may be disclosed. . .prior to its publication in proposed form." The names of "contact people" within the agency must be published in the *Federal Register* and a reasonable time period of at least 45 days must be allowed for comments. Notices of Intent or Preambles to Notices of Proposed Rulemaking must be written in "common everyday English understandable to the general public."[5]

Since the reforms in HEW were instituted, most of the other Federal agencies have adopted policies of openness and, of course, President Carter has since directed that all Federal departments simplify regulations and invite public participation. Some would say that the success of the BEH strategy was the catalyst for the original reforms within HEW.

The BEH took several steps to involve the public in the drafting of regulations. As a first step, twenty meetings about the law were held across the nation. Both special interest and geographic factors were considered in scheduling the sessions. The Office of Education reported that some 2,200 people participated and several hundred comments were received. Approximately 170 people were chosen in June, 1976 from representatives of special interest organizations, administrators of state and local schools, and parents to par-

---

[5] Mathews Memorandum, July 26, 1976.

ticipate in a national writing group. The group developed concept papers which formed the basis for the proposed regulations. Between July and November, 1976, redrafts of these papers were prepared and comments were solicited on each version by BEH.

Proposed rules were then published in the *Federal Register* on December 30, 1976, and the public was given 60 days to comment. In addition, public hearings were held by the BEH in Washington, San Francisco, Denver, Chicago, Boston, and Atlanta. By March 1, 1977 over 16,000 written comments were received by BEH and had to be considered in the writing of the final regulations.

Other efforts were made by the Office of Education to encourage maximum public participation. A national conference on the regulations was held for administrators of state agency programs. Representatives of the BEH attended and actively participated in regional meetings and seminars held by or in conjunction with national organizations.

WRITING THE REGULATIONS — ACTION ON THE COMMENTS

When an agency is given the responsibility for administering a law, the task is two-fold. First, areas of the law which have no specific requirements about implementation of intent must be clarified. Secondly, clearly written provisions in the law must be administered on a day to day basis. In its introductory comments on the proposed rules, the Bureau explained this procedure:

> Because the statute is very comprehensive and specific on many points, the Department has elected 1) to incorporate the basic wording or substance of the Statute directly into the regulations, and 2) to expand on the statutory provisions only where additional interpretations seem to be necessary. . . .(a)n attempt has been made to

indicate (wherever possible) which requirements are statutory and which ones are regulations that attempt to interpret, clarify, or implement a specific requirement in the Act.[6]

Proposed rules were issued on December 30, 1976 and were a result of the work of the twelve writing teams convened at the national writing meeting. The concept papers were redrafted five times before being published in the *Federal Register* and interested groups were offered the opportunity to comment throughout the process. Interested persons were given until the following March 1, 1977, to comment on the proposed rules and a number of public hearings were held across the country.

Rules and regulations, certainly in the case of PL 94-142, travel through the law step by step and interpret it where necessary. Several resources are used as a basis for interpretation in addition to public comment, which together, are called the legislative history of the law. For instance, House and Senate committees frequently explain their intent in including a requirement in the law in their committee reports. Often, points are clarified further during debate on the House and Senate floor between members. Compromises reached in the Conference Committee are explained in the Conference Committee report and so on. In the final rules, published in the *Federal Register* on August 23, 1977, the Bureau of Education for the Handicapped used all these resources to explain and interpret PL 94-142. The regulations contained an *Appendix* which explained their actions taken on significant public comments and any changes which were made from the December Proposed Rules. In addition, explanatory comments were made in the text of the regulations which further explained or interpreted the rule. The following example illustrates how an agency interprets and implements a statute, in this case PL 94-142.

[6] *Federal Register*, December 30, 1976

The term "due process" means a process or procedure which is "due" a person by reason of a rule, regulation, statute, or constitutional requirement. The "due process" provisions of PL 94-142 had been a key issue during the legislative process and their importance continued during the development of the "regs" by the BEH. PL 94-142 mandated by law detailed requirements for state and local education agencies to follow in providing "due process" to handicapped children.[7] Federally-mandated "due process" requirements are looked upon at times as federal interference with state and local views of "due process," and PL 94-142's procedural requirements were the subject of a great number of public comments. According to BEH, several commenters (representing the handicapped groups) wanted even more regulations in this area while others (representing state and local government) thought that the law was specific enough and further clarification was unnecessary. The sub-part dealing with due process procedures guaranteed for parents and children includes evaluation procedures, the least restrictive environment requirements, confidentiality of information, and hearing procedures.

PL 94-142 states that parents of handicapped children must be able to obtain an independent evaluation of their child; that is, a parent may have the child evaluated by a qualified examiner who is not employed by the local school district. The regulations expanded on this provision by describing who pays for this evaluation and under what circumstances. The law requires that parents be notified in writing (in their native language) of the evaluation and placement procedures. BEH specified in the regulations what the notice should say and what responsibilities the state or local education agency has to insure that the parents understand the notice.

[7] Sec. 615, PL 94-142, "Procedural Safeguards."

In the area of testing, the law says that states must establish "nondiscriminatory" testing procedures for evaluating and placing handicapped children. BEH set forth *specific* federal guidelines for complying with this provision. For instance, tests must assess specific areas of educational need and not be only those aimed at assessing a special intelligence quota. Only persons with "applicable certification" may give the tests.

PL 94-142 requires that the public agency must afford parents the opportunity for an impartial due process hearing. BEH rules expand on several areas of the hearing process. First, the Bureau determined that since the law requires the local education agency to provide the hearing, *it* must bear the cost. In addition, although agencies are not required to pay for parents' representatives or witnesses, they must provide information about free or low cost legal and other relevant services.

Second, the federal law requires that impartial hearing officers conduct the hearings. To insure impartiality, BEH rules required that each public agency (for example, the local school board) maintain a list of persons who serve as hearing officers and which shows substantial proof of their qualifications. Parents and local school board officials were also specifically precluded from serving on such panels.

Third, the issue of hearing rights was clarified in the BEH regulations. Provisions were added in the regulations to prohibit the introduction of new evidence which had not been disclosed prior to the onset of the hearings, to allow the child to be present at the hearing and to require that the hearings be open to the public. In its discussion of this section, the BEH indicated that the procedures to be used and the openness of the hearing as well as the availability of the evidence would further serve to insure that the results of the hearing would be in the best interest of the handicapped child. See comparison of Law and "Regs."

"PROCEDURAL SAFEGUARDS

"Sec. 615. (a) Any State educational agency, any local educational agency, and any intermediate educational unit which receives assistance under this part shall establish and maintain procedures in accordance with subsection (b) through subsection (e) of this section to assure that handicapped children and their parents or guardians are guaranteed procedural safeguards with respect to the provision of free appropriate public education by such agencies and units.

"(b)(1) The procedures required by this section shall include, but shall not be limited to—

"(A) an opportunity for the parents or guardian of a handicapped child to examine all relevant records with respect to the identification, evaluation, and educational placement of the child, and the provision of a free appropriate public education to such child, and to obtain an independent educational evaluation of the child;

"(B) procedures to protect the rights of the child whenever the parents or guardian of the child are not known, unavailable, or the child is a ward of the State, including the assignment of an individual (who shall not be an employee of the State educational agency, local educational agency, or intermediate educational unit involved in the education or care of the child) to act as a surrogate for the parents or guardian;

"(C) written prior notice to the parents or guardian of the child whenever such agency or unit—
"(i) proposes to initiate or change, or
"(ii) refuses to initiate or change,
the identification, evaluation, or educational placement of the child or the provision of a free appropriate public education to the child;

"(D) procedures designed to assure that the notice required by clause (C) fully inform the parents or guardian, in the parents'

or guardian's native language, unless it clearly is not feasible to do so, of all procedures available pursuant to this section; and

"(E) an opportunity to present complaints with respect to any matter relating to the identification, evaluation, or educational placement of the child, or the provision of a free appropriate public education to such child.

"(2) Whenever a complaint has been received under paragraph (1) of this subsection, the parents or guardian shall have an opportunity for an impartial due process hearing which shall be conducted by the State educational agency or by the local educational agency or intermediate educational unit, as determined by State law or by the State educational agency. No hearing conducted pursuant to the requirements of this paragraph shall be conducted by an employee of such agency or unit involved in the education or care of the child.

"(c) If the hearing required in paragraph (2) of subsection (b) of this section is conducted by a local educational agency or an intermediate educational unit, any party aggrieved by the findings and decision rendered in such a hearing may appeal to the State educational agency which shall conduct an impartial review of such hearing. The officer conducting such review shall make an independent decision upon completion of such review.

"(d) Any party to any hearing conducted pursuant to subsections (b) and (c) shall be accorded (1) the right to be accompanied and advised by counsel and by individuals with special knowledge or training with respect to the problems of handicapped children, (2) the right to present evidence and confront, cross-examine, and compel the attendance of witnesses, (3) the right to a written or electronic verbatim record of such hearing, and (4) the right to written findings of fact and decisions (which findings and decisions shall also be transmitted to the advisory panel established pursuant to section 613(a)(12)).

FEDERAL REGISTER, VOL. 42, NO. 163—TUESDAY, AUGUST 23, 1977

IMPARTIAL DUE PROCESS HEARING (§ 121a.506)

Comment: A commenter asked that the regulations specify that the public agency must pay for the hearing.

Response: The change requested by the commenter has not been made. Since the statute requires that the public agency must afford parents an opportunity for a hearing, the agency must bear the cost of the hearing, except for paying for parents' representatives and witnesses. However, section 121a.506 has been amended to require agencies to provide parents with information about free or low-cost legal and other relevant services that are available.

IMPARTIAL HEARING OFFICER (§ 121a.507)

Comment: Commenters sought to have three-person panels, including parents, serve as the hearing officials. Some sought to allow and others sought not to allow school board officials from serving as hearing officials. Commenters also asked that lists of hearing officers be required, including their qualifications.

Response: A requirement has been added that each public agency keep a list of persons who serve as hearing officers and a statement of their qualifications. This should help to ensure that the requirement for impartiality is met. No other substantive change has been made. A three-person panel could be used under the existing rules, as long as the conditions of impartiality are met. However, a parent of the child in question and

school board officials are disqualified under section 121a.508.

HEARING RIGHTS (§ 121a.508)

Comment: Commenters disagreed as to whether hearing rights set forth in the proposed rules should be expanded or restricted. Among the additional rights sought were the right to compel the attendance of witnesses, prohibit the introduction of evidence not disclosed prior to the hearing, allow the child to be present and the hearing to be open to the public at the parents' discretion, and to specify whether the record of the hearing must be free or at reasonable cost.

Response: The section has been revised to add rights for any party to prohibit the introduction of evidence not previously disclosed to the other party and for the child to be present and the hearing to be open to the public. The purpose of hearings under this part is to ensure that handicapped children are provided free appropriate public education. Opening up the hearing and the evidence that may be presented should serve to insure that the result of a hearing will be in the best interests of the child. No provision has been added relating to cost. However, it is expected that a copy of any decision would be provided to the parent at no cost.

Figure 5. Comments and Response of BEH.

§ 121a.506 Impartial due process hearing.

(a) A parent or a public educational agency may initiate a hearing on any of the matters described in § 121a.504(a)(1) and (2).

(b) The hearing must be conducted by the State educational agency or the public agency directly responsible for the education of the child, as determined under State statute, State regulation, or a written policy of the State educational agency.

(c) The public agency shall inform the parent of any free or low-cost legal and other relevant services available in the area if:

(1) The parent requests the information; or

(2) The parent or the agency initiates a hearing under this section.

(20 U.S.C. 1416(b)(2).)

Comment: Many States have pointed to the success of using mediation as an intervening step prior to conducting a formal due process hearing. Although the process of mediation is not required by the statute or these regulations, an agency may wish to suggest mediation in disputes concerning the identification, evaluation, and educational placement of handicapped children, and the provision of a free appropriate public educa-

tion to those children. Mediations have been conducted by members of State educational agencies or local educational agency personnel who were not previously involved in the particular case. In many cases, mediation leads to resolution of differences between parents and agencies without the development of an adversarial relationship and with minimal emotional stress. However, mediation may not be used to deny or delay a parent's rights under this subpart.

§ 121a.507 Impartial hearing officer.

(a) A hearing may not be conducted:

(1) By a person who is an employee of a public agency which is involved in the education or care of the child, or

(2) By any person having a personal or professional interest which would conflict with his or her objectivity in the hearing.

(b) A person who otherwise qualifies to conduct a hearing under paragraph (a) of this section is not an employee of the agency solely because he or she is paid by the agency to serve as a hearing officer.

(c) Each public agency shall keep a list of the persons who serve as hearing officers. The list must include a statement of the qualifications of each of those persons.

(20 U.S.C. 1414(b)(2).)

§ 121a.508 Hearing rights.

(a) Any party to a hearing has the right to:

(1) Be accompanied and advised by counsel and by individuals with special knowledge or training with respect to the problems of handicapped children;

(2) Present evidence and confront, cross-examine, and compel the attendance of witnesses;

(3) Prohibit the introduction of any evidence at the hearing that has not been disclosed to that party at least five days before the hearing;

(4) Obtain a written or electronic verbatim record of the hearing;

(5) Obtain written findings of fact and decisions. (The public agency shall transmit those findings and decisions, after deleting any personally identifiable information, to the State advisory panel established under Subpart F).

(b) Parents involved in hearings must be given the right to:

(1) Have the child who is the subject of the hearing present; and

(2) Open the hearing to the public.

(20 U.S.C. 1415(d).)

Figure 6. Final rules and regulations of BEH. From the Federal Register, Vol. 42, No. 163, August 23, 1977, 42495. Pertaining to PL 94-142, Sec. 615 (a) (b) (c) (d).

These examples drawn from the writing of the "regs" of PL 94-142 illustrate how an agency can expand and try to clarify ambiguous areas in the language of an Act of Congress. Sometimes, however, when the agency feels there is no basis to broaden the law by extensive rule-making, it can refer to the legislative history of the bill (the debates on the floor, the House or Senate Committee Reports, etc.). "Shaky" legal issues can thus be avoided. For instance, the BEH did not want to broaden or meddle with PL 94-142's provisions for appeals of decisions made by the school board. Some of those who commented on the rules wanted parents of handicapped children to have the right to appeal such a decision directly to the courts rather than be forced to use the administrative hearing system and procedures outlined in PL 94-142. They wanted the BEH to legitimize this direct appeal to the courts if the administrative procedures were thought by parents to be futile, inadequate or untimely, or if a class action suit were involved. Their contentions were rooted in the Senate floor debate of the Senate version of the original bill (S. 6). BEH did not want to provide for this direct kind of appeal, however, because the Bureau feared far too many hearings would result in constant litigation of the school boards' decisions. To avoid meeting the commenters' desires for the direct court appeal approach, the BEH took refuge in the fact that the provision on civil actions in PL 94-142 was added in the Joint Senate-House Conference Committee, and thus, opined the BEH, it was not permissible for the BEH to use a Senate debate *which had not resulted in an amendment on the floor* as a basis for the direct court appeal method of approach. Because there was no "legitimate" legislative history providing for the direct court appeal, stated the BEH, it could not be incorporated into the "regs." The BEH further stated that in the future the problem of judicial remedies to claims of parents and handicapped children would be up to the courts to refine and resolve. Thus a "shaky" legal issue was set aside.

Interest Group Activity in Developing the Regulations

Pretty much the same groups were involved in the development of the regulations as had had a hand in the writing of PL 94-142. In fact, interest group involvement in the former was even more important. For one thing, laws passed by Congress tend to be couched in language reflective of broad policy goals and even the most specifically worded requirements must be adapted to the state and local levels. The Bureau of Education for the Handicapped, therefore, heard from state and local interest groups (such as those representing the school boards of education, state legislatures and chief state school officers etc.) about the difficulties they would have complying with the law and their suggestions for alternative strategies to carry out the law's intent without having a total disruption of the public school system. Furthermore, both the groups representing the deliverers of service (agencies of state and local government) and those representing the recipients of the services (the clients of the interest groups) scrupulously compare the language in the Act of Congress with that of the regulations. The service deliverers often complain about agency "over-regulation" and cite the letter of the Public Law to prove the federal agency is overstepping its bounds; service recipient groups will then complain about the failure of the Federal agency to regulate properly, which they perceive to be a dilution of the Public Law. So it was with the writing of the regulations for PL 94-142. Comments and suggestions were received by the BEH from all sides, and the basic issues emerged once again. The interest groups of the state and local agencies — the service-deliverers— were wary of the traditional threat, that of federal encroachment on their state and local prerogatives. They viewed themselves as protectors of "state sovereignty." The interest groups representing the handicapped were suspicious of the intentions of the former and were careful to combat any inclination of the BEH to water down the intent of the Congress to deliver a "free appropriate public education" to handicapped children throughout the country.

The State Education Agency Issue

One important issue, for example, was the administrative responsibilities of the State Education Agency (SEA) under PL 94-142. (States have different titles for their topmost education agency, all under the rubric of State Education Agency, the term used in PL 94-142.) Section 612 (6) of PL 94-142 requires that the SEA be held responsible under Federal law for assuring that

> all educational programs for handicapped children within the State, including all such programs administered by any other State or local agency, will be under the general supervision of the persons responsible for educational programs for handicapped children in the State educational agency. . . .

The Senate Committee Report on the Senate version of the bill explained this requirement further by stating that "the responsibility must remain in a central agency overseeing the education of handicapped children, so that failure to deliver services or the violation of the rights of handicapped children is squarely the responsibility of *one* agency." (italics added.)[8]

This provision was one of the aspects of PL 94-142 of which the state interest groups were wary, and they made it one of their most important priorities. They argued that in many states, several agencies — not just one — were responsible for delivering educational and other services to school-age children, whether handicapped or not, and the requirement in PL 94-142 mandated that the SEA be responsible for gen-

[8] *S. Report 94-168,* 24.

eral supervision of state agencies over which, by state law or state constitution, it had no such authority. These groups suggested that the BEH exempt states which had laws, traditional practices, or court orders which were inconsistent with this provision of PL 94-142. In addition, the states asked BEH to permit the use of interagency agreements within the states to allow for SEA supervision of other agencies providing educational services to handicapped children.

Interest groups for handicapped children, on the other hand, indicated in their comments that the regulations should set forth in clear and concise terms the responsibility and authority of the SEA over other state and local agencies servicing handicapped children regardless of the decentralization of authority in some states. Without this specific charge to the SEA's to supervise all other agencies in the state, they argued, coordinated and effective delivery of services to handicapped children would suffer needlessly. Interest groups for handicapped children thus wanted the BEH to strengthen their position in the regulations, while the states requested flexibility on their part to be in compliance with PL 94-142.

The Bureau of Education for the Handicapped fell on the side of the interest groups for handicapped children, citing both PL 94-142 itself and the Senate Committee Report as the basis for retaining the requirement in the regulations. The BEH offered several options to the states, however, which would be acceptable to the federal government for the State Education Agency to fulfill its obligations and responsibilities under the Act. If a state did not by law or constitution place full authority for delivery of educational services in a single educational agency:

1. The different state agencies could agree in writing to be monitored and bound by the SEA standards of PL 94-142;
2. The Governor of the state could establish such responsibilities by an executive directive;

3. The state could designate the SEA as the agency responsible by law or regulation.

By authorizing, in the federal regulations, these variations for the states to comply with PL 94-142's mandate that responsibility be vested in a single education agency, the BEH hoped that the law was now adapted into a practice that would be more acceptable to the States.

The Individualized Education Program (IEP)

Another important issue that concerned all interest groups was the Individualized Education Program (IEP) of Section 604 of the statute. Congress had established a comprehensive act for educating handicapped children in PL 94-142. It did not believe that a state or local education agency could subscribe to the ambitious purposes of the law unless it tailored an educational program to the specific needs of *each* handicapped child. The IEP would thus be an instrument for outlining each child's educational needs and the services required to meet them. The handicapped child was entitled to a "free appropriate public education" under the law, and the IEP would be a written document for determining just what was indeed appropriate and what kinds of services would be delivered by the education agency to fit into the proper degree of "appropriateness" for that particular handicapped child. Because the IEP was the *only* written document to evolve from the process, state and local education agencies wanted to know two things. Was the IEP a legally binding document, a contract as it were, which might subject them to a court suit brought by parents if, in the eyes of the parents, promised services were not one hundred per cent delivered; or for that matter there was disagreement about the degree of quality of the delivered services? And, did the IEP mean that the education agency guaranteed that each handicapped child would actually fully attain the goals and aims of his or her IEP? The statute specifies that the Individualized Education Program for each handicapped child *must* include such components as:

1. A statement of the child's present levels of educational performance;
2. A statement of annual goals including short-term instructional objectives;
3. A statement of the specific special education and related services to be provided to the child and the extent to which the child will be able to participate in regular educational programs (in other words, how far "mainstreaming" shall go, or just exactly what was the "least restrictive environment" for the handicapped child);
4. Schedules for review, at least annually, of the achievement of the short-term objectives.

The commitment of the education agency at the local school district level to the provisions of the IEP was substantial. State and local education agencies and their interest groups thus concentrated their efforts on minimizing any misconceptions about the legal nature of the IEP. The proposed rules stated that the IEP must list the services necessary to meet the child's needs "without regard to the availability of those services."[9] Obviously teachers of special education were in short supply, "regular" teachers were not trained to cope with all the needs of a handicapped child and for that matter with the wide variety of handicaps in a "regular" classroom, and not all services (such as special transportation equipment and wheelchairs etc.) were immediately available. All these things took time to obtain and of course cost a great deal of money. The federal government was not going to supply all the funds necessary for these things, but

[9] *Federal Register*, December 28, 1976, 56986.

only some of them and then only by way of a formula designed to help the states and local education agencies meet the "excess costs." Furthermore, if the IEP were a legally binding contract between the schools and the parents, any failure to meet the goals or deliver the services outlined in the plan became the basis of an adversary proceeding, itself an expensive matter for the education agencies.

The interest groups for the handicapped thrust such arguments aside as inconsequential and made several suggestions designed to underscore the mandatory nature of the IEP such as: having a timetable for meetings between schools and parents to develop the IEP, clarifying terms that could be misunderstood, and assuring that the parents of the handicapped child understood the procedures and objectives of the IEP.

The BEH then maintained that the proposed rules reflected the intent of the Congress and used a statement by then Congressman Albert Quie (R–Minn.), ranking Republican on the House Education and Labor Committee, as the basis for its interpretation. During the House debate on the bill, Quie stated:

> It is important to point out that (the individualized education program) is an educational program developed jointly, but it is *not* intended as a binding contract by the schools, children and parents. (Italics added)[10]

BEH concluded, therefore, that while the state or local education agency is responsible for providing the services in the IEP because it took part in its development, it is not legally responsible for failure in performance of the handicapped child.

But state and local agencies wanted further clarification, especially concerning the commitment of services which might or might not be available to the handicapped child. The costs of litigation were one thing, but the costs of

[10] *Ibid.*, 56970.

supplying "everything" were even more of a problem to them. They still wanted assurance that the IEP was only a planning document, a guideline and not a contract. In deference to them, therefore, the BEH eliminated the reference cited above to the "availability of those services". In essence, the regulations concerning the intent of the IEP were thus pruned to statutory language.

These examples illustrate how an agency uses legislative history to write the regulations, how comments from interested groups are addressed and how it determines where additional clarifications or requirements are necessary and appropriate.

While the BEH and OCR of the Department of Health, Education and Welfare were coping with the writing of the regulations for both Section 504 of PL 93–112 and PL 94–142, the 95th Congress was also at work at legislation dealing with the problems of handicapped children. Two sets of hearings occurred in 1977 which affected programs for educating handicapped children. One was on the extension of certain discretionary programs and to eliminate the National Advisory Committee on Handicapped Children. These hearings resulted in passage of PL 95–49 in June, 1977. The other set was oversight hearings on PL 94–142 in September, 1977, in which the interest groups for handicapped children and the state and local education agencies vied with one another before House and Senate Subcommittees about the efficacy of PL 94–142. (See Figure 7 for complete flowchart.)

Figure 7. Flow Chart, Development of PL 94-142.

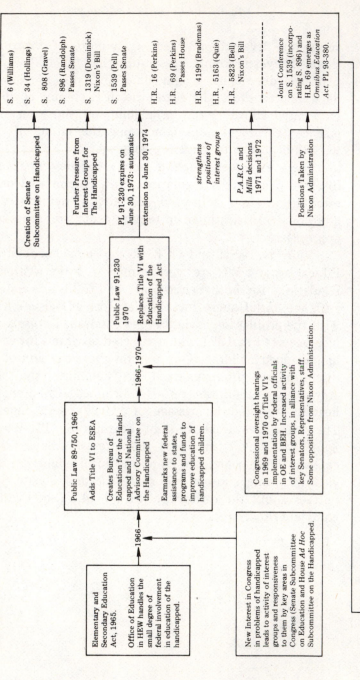

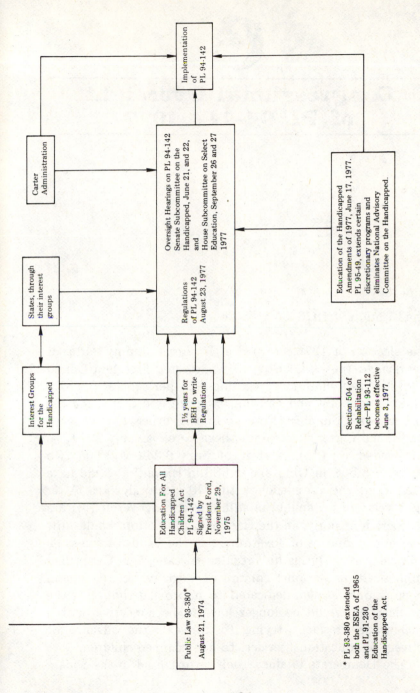

Implementation of PL 94-142

Carter Administration

Oversight Hearings on PL 94-142 Senate Subcommittee on the Handicapped, June 21, and 22, and House Subcommittee on Select Education, September 26 and 27 1977

Education of the Handicapped Amendments of 1977, June 17, 1977. PL 95-49, extends certain discretionary programs and eliminates National Advisory Committee on the Handicapped.

States, through their interest groups

Regulations of PL 94-142 August 23, 1977

Interest Groups for the Handicapped

1½ years for BEH to write Regulations

Section 504 of Rehabilitation Act—PL 93-112 becomes effective June 3, 1977

Education For All Handicapped Children Act PL 94-142 Signed by President Ford, November 29, 1975

Public Law 93-380* August 21, 1974

* PL 93-380 extended both the ESEA of 1965 and PL 91-230 Education of the Handicapped Act.

6

Congressional Oversight of PL 94-142, 1977

The Election of 1976

The election of 1976 returned a Democrat, Jimmy Carter of Georgia, to the White House. He defeated President Gerald Ford in a very close race, winning 50.1 per cent of the 81.5 million votes cast and carrying twenty-three States and the District of Columbia. Ford won the other twenty-seven States, and Carter's electoral college vote was only 297 (270 are needed to win). A shift of only 9,244 votes in two States — 5,558 in Ohio and 3,686 in Hawaii — would have given Ford the Presidency with 270 electoral votes. After eight years of a Republican administration governing with a Democratic majority in the Congress, the nation would now have both branches of government in the hands of the same political party. During his Presidential campaign, Carter had emphasized his personal commitment to human rights, and Congressional leaders dedicated to improving the lot of the handicapped would no longer have to be concerned with a recalcitrant President trying to forestall the advance of delivery of educational services to handicapped children.

The Democrats retained their strong hold in the Senate

and House, continuing their 62 per cent majority in the Senate and their 67 per cent majority in the House. Democratic leadership of Senate and House subcommittees dealing with handicapped legislation remained the same. Senator Jennings Randolph continued to chair the Senate Subcommittee on the Handicapped, and Representative John Brademas, who became House Majority Whip in 1977, held the leadership of the House Subcommittee on Select Education. Republican Senator Robert Stafford, who firmly adhered to the same principles as Randolph, remained the ranking Republican on the Senate subcommittee. Republican membership on the House subcommittee continued uneven with no one holding continuous service on it. Nevertheless, Republicans and Democrats on the House subcommittee were just as non-partisan in their approach to the handicapped issue as were those on the Senate side, and the staff of both Senate and House subcommittees remained stable. The interest groups for handicapped children continued to have their "friends" in key positions in the 95th Congress.

The Senate had done some reshuffling of the Committee structure by 1977 (some called it reform). The Labor and Public Welfare Committee, the parent committee of the Subcommittee on the Handicapped, had been renamed the Human Resources Committee in 1977 and later became the Labor and Human Resources Committee. The membership of the Subcommittee on the Handicapped was reduced in size to three Democrats and two Republicans in 1977-1978. Williams, the Chairman of the full committee and who had served on the Handicapped Subcommittee *ex officio* throughout its short history, now became a full member of the Subcommittee as did Eagleton. State representation on both the Senate and House Subcommittees remained pretty much the same, with a strong emphasis on those States with the most handicapped children.[1]

---

[1] See pages 134–135.

Public Law 95-49, 1977 (Extension of Authorization for Support Services)

In the first six months of 1977, while the Bureau of Education for the Handicapped was working on the regulations for PL 94-142, the Congress dealt with another aspect of educating handicapped children. It must be realized that PL 94-142 was a landmark Act providing for the writing into federal law the concept that all handicapped children were entitled to a "free appropriate public education." It was not an authorization for providing for the support services necessary to help the States educate handicapped children. Congressional authorization for these — the continuance and expansion of regional resource centers and services to meet the needs of handicapped children and the provision for research, instructional media and the training of personnel for educating handicapped children — was rooted in PL 91-230 (1970) and PL 93-380 (1974). Federal funds for these programs now had to be reauthorized if the goal of full service to all handicapped children by September 1, 1980, as required by PL 94-142, was to be met. Accordingly, S. 725 and H.R. 6692 became the vehicles for their continuance and provided once again a platform for the interest groups concerned with handicapped children and their education.

Composition of Senate and House Subcommittees Dealing with Handicapped, 1973-1980

Senate Subcommittee on Handicapped		*House Subcommittee on Select Education*	
Democrats	*Republicans*	*Democrats*	*Republicans*
93rd Congress, 1973-1974			
Randolph (W.Va.), *Chair*	Stafford (Vt.) Taft (Ohio)	Brademas (Ind.), *Chair*	Eshleman (Pa.) Landgrebe (Ind.)

Cranston (Calif.)   Schweiker (Pa.) Mink (Hawaii)   Hansen (Idaho)
Williams (N.J.)   Beall (Md.)   Meeds (Wash.)   Peyser (N.Y.)
Pell (R.I.)   Chisholm (N.Y.)   Sarasin (Conn.)
Kennedy (Mass.)   Grasso (Conn.)
Mondale (Minn.)   Mazzoli (Ky.)
Hathaway (Maine)   Badillo (N.Y.)
                                       Lehman (Fla.)

94th Congress, 1975–1976

Randolph (W.Va.),   Stafford (Vt.)   Brademas (Ind.)   Bell (Calif.)
  Chair   Taft (Ohio)   *Chair*   Peyser (N.Y.)
Cranston (Calif.)   Schweiker (Pa.) Mink (Hawaii)   Jeffords (Vt.)
Pell (R.I.)   Beall (Md.)   Meeds (Wash.)   Pressler (S.Dak.)
Kennedy (Mass.)   Chisholm (N.Y.)
Mondale (Minn.)   Lehman (Fla.)
Hathaway (Maine)   Cornell (Wisc.)
                                       Beard (R.I.)
                                       Zeferetti (N.Y.)
                                       Miller (Calif.)
                                       Hall (Ill.)

95th Congress, 1977–78

Randolph (W.Va.),   Stafford (Vt.)   Brademas (Ind.), Jeffords (Vt.)
  Chair   Hatch (Utah)   *Chair*   Pressler (S.Dak.)
Williams (N.J.)   Beard (R.I.)
Eagleton (Mo.)   Miller (Calif.)
                                       Kildee (Mich.)
                                       Heftel (Hawaii)
                                       Hawkins (Calif.)
                                       Biaggi (N.Y.)

96th Congress, 1979–1980

Randolph (W.Va.),   Stafford (Vt.)   Simon (Ill.),   Kramer (Colo.)
  Chair   Schweiker (Pa.)   *Chair*   Coleman (Mo.)
Eagleton (Mo.)   Brademas (Ind.), Erdahl (Minn.)
Riegle (Mich.)   *Whip*
                                       Beard (R.I.)
                                       Miller (Calif.)
                                       Hawkins (Calif.)
                                       Biaggi (N.Y.)
                                       Stack (Fla.)

It was taken for granted by all concerned that the Congress would extend the programs for support services and authorize funds, so the hearings on S. 725 and H.R. 6692 really focussed on the problems of educating handicapped children as they then existed. One thing was apparent in both

House and Senate Subcommittee hearings. There was an increased political presence of state and local education agencies before the subcommittees. They used these hearings and those that were to follow in late June and September to combat what they believed to be were their growing concerns about the efficacy of federal involvement and regulation in the education of handicapped children. They were also immersed in the process that the BEH was going through in writing the "regs" for PL 94-142 and wanted to emphasize their opinions before the Congressional committees. Interest groups for handicapped children, who were also pressing their views on the BEH, realized the difficulties they might face in the growing reluctance of some state and local education agencies to carry out fully the intent of federal legislation and seized the opportunity to stress again the importance of federal involvement and to counteract the threat of serious opposition stemming from state and local education agencies.

Senate Subcommittee on The Handicapped, Hearings on S. 725, 1977

The Senate subcommittee held hearings on S. 725 within a general review of programs for the handicapped beginning on February 7 through March 22, 1977.[2] More than 30 witnesses testified in support of the extension of the discretionary programs authorized by S. 725.[3] Like the House hearings

[2] Hearings on *Review of Programs for the Handicapped, 1977,* Senate Subcommittee on the Handicapped, 95th Cong., 1st Sess., Parts 1, 2 and 3, February 7, 8, 24, 25, 28 and March 2, 21 and 22, 1977.

[3] Among those testifying, representing groups for the handicapped were the National Consortium on Physical Education and Recreation for the Handicapped, American Speech and Hearing Association, Center on Deafness at the California State University, Program for the Deaf at Seattle Community College, Louisiana Program for the Deaf, Council for Exceptional Children, Epilepsy Foundation of America, National Association of Retarded Citizens, United Cerebral Palsy Association,

on its counterpart, H.R. 6692, that were to take place later in April and May, there was general agreement in the Senate hearings that the programs supplying federal funds for regional resource centers and services, research, instructional media and training of personnel for special education should be extended and funded. Chairman Jennings Randolph took great delight in pointing out that the Carter Administration, unlike that of Nixon and Ford, was completely committed to increasing federal expenditures in the sphere of educating handicapped children.[4]

State and local education agencies also expressed their views that even more Federal funds than S. 725 would authorize were needed if the difficulties in educating handicapped children were to be overcome. Some of them, however, also stressed a general uneasiness about federal rules that might well upset the delicate relationship between federal, state, and local government. Much of the information given to the Senate subcommittee concerned the advances that individual states had already made in bringing educational services to their handicapped children.

The handicapped interest groups not only supported S. 725 but also began their assault on the state and local education agencies and teacher organizations which they believed would drag their feet as time went on in properly counting all their handicapped children, developing comprehensive individualized education programs, and placing handicapped children in the least restrictive environment possible. They

---

American Foundation for the Blind, National Easter Seal Society for Crippled Children Association of Children with Learning Disabilities. Among those representing State and local education agencies and teacher groups were the National Association of State Directors of Special Education (NASDE), Minnesota State Director of Special Education, Massachusetts State Director of Special Education, Missouri Department of Elementary and Secondary Education, Vermont Department of Education, American Federation of Teachers, National Education Association and the Indiana State Education Teachers Association.

[4] *Ibid.*, p. 799.

would later develop this theme in the House subcommittee hearings on H.R. 6692 and the oversight hearings on PL 94-142 conducted by the House Subcommittee on Select Education and the Senate Subcommittee on the Handicapped.

House Subcommittee on Select Education Hearings on H.R. 6692, 1977.

The House Subcommittee held its hearings in Washington on April 25 and May 2, 1977[5] taking testimony from several interest groups representing the handicapped and groups representing various State and local education agencies, project centers, and teacher organizations.[6] The Carter Administration sent Mary Berry, Assistant Secretary of Education in HEW and Edwin Martin, head of the BEH. All the groups urged the House subcommittee to approve the authorization to extend the discretionary programs but the interest groups for handicapped children, led by the Council for Exceptional Children, took center stage before Brademas' sympathetic subcommittee.

First, the CEC requested more programs to include the nation's gifted and talented children who, after all, were just as "handicapped" in a regular classroom as were the physically and mentally handicapped. CEC argued that there were

[5] Hearings on *Extension of the Education of the Handicapped Act*, House Subcommittee on Select Education, 95th Con., 1st Sess., April 25 and May 2, 1977.

[6] Among those in the first group were Council for Exceptional Children, National Association of Retarded Citizens, National Consortium on Physical Education and Recreation for the Handicapped, American Speech and Hearing Association, Program for the Deaf, American Foundation for the Blind, American Speech and Hearing Association. Among the second group were Program for Severely Handicapped Children and Youth, Madison Wisconsin Public Schools, Texas Education Agency, New York State Education Department, Oklahoma Childrens Services Demonstration Center, University of Pittsburgh Special Education Department, American Federation of Teachers.

only 2.5 million federal dollars available for them, although twenty-seven states had some sort of program. The Council also sought to have the name of the BEH changed to the Bureau of Education for Exceptional Persons, thus covering both handicapped and gifted children.[7] Aware that many local education agencies, school boards, parents of "normal" children, and teachers in the public schools were becoming wary of PL 94–142 requirements that handicapped children be placed in the regular classroom wherever appropriate, CEC took the opportunity to underscore the need for having these children in the least restrictive environment possible. The term "mainstreaming" was beginning to become a euphemism for this approach to educating handicapped children and indeed a red flag for many, who feared that having handicapped children mixed in with "normal" children would have an ill effect on the education of the latter. The CEC position, and that of the interest groups for handicapped children, was that placing handicapped children in the "mainstream" of their peers would help not only the handicapped to learn to cope with the non-handicapped world of their own age group, but also the "normal" children would benefit from the experience. It was educational for both handicapped and non-handicapped to learn together wherever possible. After all, in the new age of civil rights, it would hardly do for one group to argue against being integrated with another just because one of them was "different." True enough, there were physical and logistical problems to work out, but CEC believed that these should be overcome. The financial cost of placing children in the least restrictive environment available was no excuse for not doing so. It had not been an excuse in the desegregation of the public schools when it came to racial differences, it ought not to be when it came to physical and mental differences. Reacting to public misinformation about "mainstreaming," the CEC attacked teacher organiza-

[7]House Subcommittee Hearings, op.cit., 5, 23 and 48.

tions, like the American Federation of Teachers, which disagreed with this method of implementing the goals of educating handicapped children. The AFT was concerned that "mainstreaming" requirements (due process hearings were required to determine whether or not a handicapped child could or could not be "mainstreamed") put undue safety burdens on teachers and heavy burdens on them to develop an individualized education program for each handicapped child. The AFT argued that PL 94-142 carried no due process protection for the teachers.[8] CEC, in response, stated that the AFT's "emotional concern" had no factual basis, and it was time to change the attitudes of such people who were engaging in "scare tactics" about "mainstreaming." To do this, the Council pointed out that parents of handicapped children should put more pressure on the schools to overcome the dilatory tactics of school superintendents[9] who were not disposed to taking on the American Federation of Teachers on the issue of "mainstreaming." The Council stated that "mainstreaming" simply means placing the handicapped child in the least restrictive environment. The purpose of this provision of PL 94-142 was to keep school agencies from placing handicapped children in inadequate, unsatisfactory, and unequal conditions and thus sweeping handicapped children under the school district rug. No handicapped child ought to be restricted "because of a label that might be placed on that child."[10] The President of the CEC, Harold Perry, said:

> To say that we are going to put every retarded child, every learning disability child, every emotionally disturbed child, into a regular classroom full time is foolish, first of all; it is incorrect, most of all.[11]

[8] *Ibid.*, 64-68.
[9] *Ibid.*, 29.
[10] *Ibid.*, 31.
[11] *Ibid.*

This was the general line taken by the pro-handicapped children groups. They were reserving their ammunition, however, for the Senate and House oversight hearings on PL 94–142 that were due to start the following month in June. The state and local education agencies of course continued to urge further extension and funding of the discretionary programs and they too were waiting for the congressional hearings on oversight.

Provisions of PL 95-49, Education of the Handicapped Amendments of 1977

The Senate Committee on Human Resources and House Committee on Education and Labor, the parent committees of the subcommittees, reported out almost identical bills on May 6, 1977. The House passed the bill on May 9, and the Senate passed it on May 23, with a slight amendment. The House then concurred on June 7 and the bill became Public Law 95-49 when President Carter approved it on June 17, 1977.

The Act extended for five years federal support for:

Regional Resource Centers — authorizing $19 million for fiscal 1978, increasing to $25 million by fiscal 1982.

Centers and Services for deaf-blind children — authorizing $22 million for fiscal year 1978, increasing to $32 million by fiscal 1982.

Pre-school Education for Handicapped Children — $25 million for fiscal 1978, decreasing to $20 million by fiscal 1982.

Regional Education Programs — $10 million for fiscal 1978, increasing to $16 million by fiscal 1982.

The Training of Teachers of Special Education — $75 million for fiscal 1978, increasing to $95 million in fiscal 1982.

Research in Educating Handicapped Children — $20 million for fiscal 1978, increasing to $28 million for fiscal 1982.
Instructional Media — $24 million for fiscal 1978, increasing to $29 million by fiscal 1982.

These were authorizations for appropriations, and whether future Congresses would actually appropriate full funding, remained to be seen. (We shall deal with the problem of appropriations in the next chapter.)

Believing that the Bureau of Education for the Handicapped was now providing effective leadership in the education of the handicapped, the Congress eliminated in PL 94–49 provisions for the continuation of the National Advisory Committee on the Handicapped.

We now turn to the 1977 Congressional oversight hearings on PL 94-142.

Congressional Oversight Hearings on PL 94-142, 1977

Four days after PL 95–49 had been approved, with the BEH still putting final touches on the regulations for PL 94–142, the Senate Subcommittee on The Handicapped began two days of oversight hearings on the Education for All Handicapped Children Act in June.[12] PL 94-142 was not due to go into effect until October 1, 1977, but the Subcommittee felt it should hold hearings to see what progress was being made "to bring the States to compliance with the law so that each handicapped child across the nation [would] have the protections guaranteed" by PL 94-142 and the Constitution.[13] Senator Harrison Williams, chairman of the parent

[12] Hearings, *Education for All Handicapped Children Act, 1977.* Senate Subcommittee on the Handicapped, 95th Cong., 1st Sess., June 21 and 22, 1977.
[13] *Ibid.*, 30.

Human Resources Committee, saw no reason to amend PL 94-142 so early in the process, but realized there were many issues about its implementation that various states and interest groups for the handicapped wanted to air.[14]

Now that PL 94-142 was "in place" the concerns of the states and local education agencies were quite different from those of the handicapped interest groups. They both wanted federal assistance, but the interest groups for the handicapped wanted to stress the vital importance of full implementation of the law while state and local education agencies who, along with the teachers in the country, were the deliverers of services to handicapped children, wanted to point out to the subcommittee, and to its House counterpart later in September, the great difficulties facing them in that implementation.

In September, one month after the regulations for PL 94-142 had been promulgated, the House Subcommittee on Select Education held a similar set of hearings for two days.[15] The division of those giving testimony before the House subcommittee into two panels, one representing the deliverers of education services and the other the interest groups for handicapped children, reflected the suspicion between the two sides that was developing over the implementation of PL 94-142. While handicapped legislation was growing in importance between 1966 and 1975, there was no serious opposition to the concept from any source. Indeed, the states had welcomed more federal assistance in the area, although, given their experiences in other types of grant-in-aid programs, they were doubtlessly wary of the potential consequences of such legislation. Now that PL 94-142 was "in place," they went public to emphasize their forebodings about the potential impact on their sovereignty of

---

[14] *Ibid.*

[15] Hearings, *Education for All Handicapped Children Act*, House Subcommittee on Select Education, 95th Cong., 1st Sess., September 26 and 27, 1977.

full implementation of the law. The interest groups for the handicapped were not confident that the state and local education agencies would exercise their greatest efforts to see to it that handicapped children did indeed receive the "free appropriate public education" to which they were entitled. Now that they had obtained their long–sought federal legislation and had seen some of the opposition stemming from the SEA's and LEA's in the writing of the "regs," they realized they had to push the states even harder. They too went public before the House subcommittee to resist what they feared was growing opposition to full implementation of PL 94–142.

Since the hearings by both subcommittees covered the same ground and testimony of both sides were similar in both, we shall treat the oversight hearings together. Eighteen groups representing the positions of several states, state education agencies, and teacher organizations testified or placed their comments on the record as did twelve groups concerned with delivering full education services to handicapped children. They are as follows:

Representing the first group: Massachusetts, Pennsylvania, Florida, New York, Texas, Iowa, Illinois, Missouri, West Virginia, Washington, California, National Conference of State Legislatures, National Governors' Conference, National Association of State Boards of Education, National School Boards of Education, Education Commission of the States, Council of Chief State School Officers, and the National Education Association.

Representing the second group: Children's Defense Fund, Council for Exceptional Children, American Coalition of Citizens with Disabilities, American Friends Service Committee, Public Education Associates of New York, Massachusetts Advocacy Center, National Association for Retarded Citizens, American Occupational Therapy Association, Center for Independent Living, Association for Children with Learning Disabilities, Southwestern Ohio

Coalition for Handicapped Children, and Voice for the Handicapped, Inc.

Seven areas of practical importance emerged from the Senate and House Subcommittee Hearings in June and September. Settlement of the issues attendant to the areas was essential for the success of PL 94-142, and they would serve as pivotal focal points for delivery of a "free appropriate public education" and services necessary for that delivery to handicapped children in the next two years.

Appropriations

Although we shall deal later with the matter of the actual appropriations in relation to the authorization of funds by PL 94-142, suffice it to point out here that both groups were in accord that the funds authorized were insufficient to accomplish what PL 94-142 set out to do. The chief executives of the states, through their own pressure group, the National Governors' Conference (now called the National Governors' Association), expressed their strong desire to have the federal government guarantee full reimbursement for the cost of all students enrolled in special education programs. Although this aim was unrealistic, New York and Texas representatives urged it as well. The Education Commission of the States, another important pressure group of the states, wanted Congress to amend PL 94-142 by doing away with the concept that only state "excess costs" for educating handicapped children would be in part funded by the federal government. The ECS wanted the states to have the right to comingle federal and state funds (thus making it difficult for the federal government to monitor whether or not federal funds were being used to the best advantage) or even have federal funds supplant or replace altogether state expenditures.[16] The National Conferences of State Legislatures' witness went even further in his testimony before the House Subcommittee. He argued that the amount of money required to educate handicapped children varied from State to State. (The subcommittees were often reminded about the nature of diversity within the federal system of government.) Under PL 94-142, states that were already heavily committed in dollars to their handicapped children's education would receive relatively *fewer* federal dollars than the less committed states. Thus PL 94-142 treated them unfairly because of their early commitment to relieving the plight of handicapped children. They were being penalized for that early concern rather than being rewarded. They wanted to have the right, therefore, to use Federal funds to supplant some of their already committed state funds. States which were underfunded, however, and needed a massive new commitment because of PL 94-142, required many more federal dollars to begin with than did the other states. Hence, they wanted Federal funds to cover a higher proportion of "excess costs" than PL 94-142 allocated.[17] Complementing this argument was that of the National Association of State Boards of Education (NASBE), which pointed out that the new commitment of state funds would mean that much state money would be taken away from "regular education programs to fulfill the needs of special education programs." (This was an argument that would be stressed time and time again at the local school district level, not only by the local education agencies, but also by parents of "normal" children.) NASBE wanted the 40 per cent formula of allocation to be applied right away rather than in fiscal 1982 as PL 94-142 mandated.[18]

There was no chance that the Congress would ever con-

[16] Senate Subcommittee Hearings, 331-357.

[17] House Subcommittee Hearings, 3.

[18] *Ibid.*, 32.

sider full funding of the education for handicapped programs. Nor would the Congress supply federal money beyond the "excess costs" concept that it had incorporated into PL 94-142. The interest groups for handicapped children, therefore, were not overly concerned that the Congress would pay any attention to the requests the States were making in this regard. They asked Congress, through the subcommittees, only to consider raising the authorizations for appropriations and to make as certain as possible that the promises made for the mandated levels of authorizations would be kept in the near future.

Pass-Through Funds

The concept of providing "pass-through" funds had evolved from the revenue-sharing plans rooted in the Johnson Administration and developed more fully during the Nixon years as a means of distributing some federal funds, raised through federal taxation, to the states and localities for various types of projects. The usual method of distributing federal funds is tied (and has been for some time) to a categorical grant-in-aid program of one sort or another wherein the federal government puts up a certain percentage of funds for a project or program and the state the remainder. This kind of federal grant policy has been applied to highway construction, health and welfare programs, and urban development among other projects. To receive federal funds, however, the state not only has to put up a share of the costs of the project, but also has to satisfy federal rules and regulations designed to ensure that federal funds are not spent improperly. States often feel that the federal government thereby has "strings" on them, and the entity that controls the "strings" has a decided impact on policy-making in the long run. These "strings" annoy most of the states who often react strongly to federal overseeing *their* ways of doing things (a reflection once again of the nature of diversity in the federal system of government) and to the excessive amount of paperwork required to satisfy the federal agency to which the state is accountable. Local government, as well, often has the same attitude toward the state as the state has toward the federal government, because the state imposes the same sort of "strings" for state aid to the locality as the federal government imposes on the state. Local governments, particularly the cities, dissatisfied with this arrangement and unhappy over the small amount of funds they were receiving from the state, turned to Washington and the Congress in the 1960's for some Federal funds outside of the categorical grant-in-aid system which would bypass the states and "feed" the localities directly. Congressional response was the development of a modest revenue-sharing program during the Nixon Administration, a system whereby a small but specific percentage of federal aid to the states is "passed–through" the state directly to local government for dispersion for local projects. The "pass-through" arrangement of PL 94–142, therefore, had a recent history, and state education agencies feared that with the direct pass-through of 75 per cent authorized by PL 94–142 they would eventually lose control of education policy. The local education agencies, naturally, differed with the state education agencies on this issue. The states wanted federal funds mandated by PL 94–142 to be allocated *by the states* according to each individual state formula for its special education assistance program. They argued that the states had widespread diversity in the way they equalized financial differences among the various localities within each State. State fund allocation is often higher in localities which have a low tax base and lower where the locality has a high tax base (as in a school district with high property values and thereforth with more property taxes to tap for local schools).

The interest groups for the handicapped welcomed the pass-through system and expressed their satisfaction with the method of allocation. When local education agencies complained of the sums of money required to carry out the mandates of PL 94-142, the interest groups could always point to the fact that the federal government was supplying at least some of that money without the LEA's having to be concerned with State dictation.

The Handicapped Children Count

Under terms of PL 94-142, the states had to have a timetable for identifying their handicapped children and had to count how many were actually receiving services from the State. The latter count was to be made twice during the school year, on October 1 and February 1, with the average of the two counts then used as the official number for the application of the financial formula for allocation of federal funds. A multi-handicapped child (and there were many) was to be counted only once. The states did not believe they could identify all their handicapped children within the timetable, nor did they have the money — so they said — that such a count would cost. This objection was made by the states of Pennsylvania, Florida, New York; the National Conference of State Legislatures; the Council of Chief State School Officers; and the National Association of State Boards of Education. They also wanted each child counted as many times as the child received services for each handicap and the count to be made on the basis of daily membership in the classroom. Not to do so would result, they claimed, in an undercount of handicapped children. (Massachusetts, The National Governors' Conference, and the Education Commission of the States).

The interest groups for handicapped children strongly opposed these arguments (the chief responsibility for carrying their view was placed in the Council for Exceptional Children) before both subcommittees. They wanted the child counted only once (believing that the states would purposely undercount the number of children entitled to services if the multiple count system was employed, thus not having to spend as much state money as compliance with PL 94-142 would then require). They also argued that taking the average number of children being served, as counted twice a year, would result in a higher count because handicapped children could not always be in full attendance. By counting them in October and February and then averaging those counts, they felt that a more accurate reflection of children being served would result in forcing the States to serve these children more completely. The Council for Exceptional Children had its own set of statistics as to how many handicapped children there were in the nation and did not trust the states' versions. By counting as many as possible, the CEC believed that the desire of some states to play down the count and carry out the mandate of PL 94-142 as little as possible would be thwarted.

State Education Agency Responsibility

The requirement of Section 612(6) of PL 94-142 that:

The State education agency shall be responsible for assuring that the requirements of this part are carried out and that all educational programs for handicapped children within the State, including all such programs administered by any other State or local agency, will be under the general supervision of the persons responsible for educational programs for handicapped children in the State educational agency and shall meet education standards of the State educational agency

was particularly an anethma to the states. They viewed this provision as another example of federal encroachment on the sovereign right of states to administer their affairs as they saw fit and as contrary to laws and constitutions of several states.

The state education agencies in New Hampshire, Colorado, Wyoming and Louisiana had limited authority under state law or constitution over the operations of local school districts. Section 612(6) did not take into account the diversity of the states in methods of finance and governance. (National Governors Conference.) They wanted PL 94–142 amended to permit each state to have its own system of responsibility for making the local education agencies accountable for carrying out the provisions and mandates of the law. (Education Commission of the States.)

The interest groups for handicapped children came out very strongly in both sets of hearings in favor of retaining Section 612(6) as written by statute. Vesting control of and accountability for the state's plans in the state education agency would avoid the common occurrence whereby some states avoided responsibility for handicapped children by shunting responsibility from a State Department of Mental Health, to Vocational Rehabilitation Agencies, to education agencies, to public welfare bureaus etc. (Childrens Defense Fund), thus letting handicapped children "fall between the cracks." This was no way to deliver full educational services to handicapped children (National Association for Retarded Citizens). The states' argument against the SEA requirement was shallow. The Council for Exceptional Children stated that the reality is "that state agencies do not want to work together, and that they do not want to give up their own little turfs." Doing away with the SEA position of authority in the states meant that handicapped children would "get lost between the bureaucratic shuffle of state and local agencies."[19] In general the interest groups for handicapped children were adamant in their defense of the SEA provisions of PL 94–142. Without enforcing the responsibility on the state education agency as outlined in the law, a "free appropriate public education" would not be delivered to the nation's handicapped children.

[19] Senate Subcommittee Hearings, 72.

Individualized Education Program (IEP)

Throughout the decade prior to pasage of PL 94-142 proponents of the "free appropriate public education" concept assumed that every handicapped child could and should be educated to the fullest extent possible within his or her uppermost capabilities. Otherwise the handicapped child would never reach a condition of self-sufficiency. Section 614 (a) (5) of the law mandated that each handicapped child being served have an Individualized Education Program tailored to his or her specific needs at the beginning of every school year. The local education agency was also directed by law to review and, if appropriate, revise the IEP at least annually. The states were much concerned that they would be simply unable to cater to every handicapped child being served in the school systems. Pennsylvania, for example, pointed out that PL 94-142 required that parents be directly included in the procedures establishing the IEP, but Pennsylvania's education program for handicapped children specifically omitted such a role for parents in their agency procedures.[20] One particular concern of the states, as had emerged in the writing of the regulations, was the legal nature of the IEP. The states feared that once an IEP was written for a handicapped child, the local education agency would be legally bound to guarantee that the child would actually reach the goals set by the IEP. The Bureau of Education for the Handicapped's assurance that the IEP was not a legally binding contract but only a guideline was unacceptable to the Education Commission of the States (ECS) which wanted PL 94-142 amended to state flatly that the IEP was only a plan, not a contract. The States were leery that without such statutory language in the law, the courts might well rule that it was a contract, thereby making the states and the local education agencies liable for damages in a suit brought by

[20] *Ibid.*, 97.

parents of a handicapped child who did not reach the goals set by the IEP. According to the Council of Chief State School Officers, the IEP requirement could thus lead to an overabundance of litigation.

The interest groups for the handicapped confronted the states headlong on the IEP issue. The Childrens Defense Fund claimed the IEP procedures were necessary to keep some states from mislabeling culturally deprived children as mentally retarded. Furthermore, if a handicapped child has the right under PL 94-142 to a "free appropriate public education" and related services, the IEP must be binding on the local education agency, otherwise the Education for All Handicapped Children Act would be "meaningless and unenforceable."[21] The Council for Exceptional Children stated that the IEP was the critical link in PL 94-142 "between children's needs and what is going to be provided for them." The IEP, said the spokesman for the CEC, was indeed a contract to provide services to the handicapped, not a contract that guaranteed "what we hope the child will learn has to be achieved."[22] In answer to the reluctance on the part of Pennsylvania to include parents in the writing of the IEP, the Southwestern Ohio Coalition Parent Information group said that such inclusion was necessary because the IEP was the promise that the school will deliver the services as agreed upon as needed. The IEP "is an opportunity for parents and professionals to sit down together for the first time to decide what is really best for the child. This is the great new chance for shared responsibility and shared commitment."[23]

It was clear in both sets of hearings that the interest groups for the handicapped believed that the local schools would have to root their future obligations to handicapped

[21] House Subcommittee Hearings, 83.

[22] *Ibid.*, 65-66.

[23] *Ibid.*, 121.

children in the IEP as prescribed by PL 94-142 and the regulations promulgated by the BEH. Only in this way could the handicapped and their parents combat the reluctance of the states to deliver full services. At least, this is the way they saw it.

The Least Restrictive Environment Issue

The requirement that handicapped children should be placed in the regular classroom wherever possible and thereby in the least restrictive environment was particularly vexing to many state and local education agencies as well as teacher organizations, not to mention parents of non-handicapped children. Many handicapped children were being treated as "different" and "strange" and therefore separated from regular schoolchildren. Or, they were simply not being educated at all. Placing them in regular classrooms, wherever possible and only if appropriate, would bring them more into the normal atmosphere in which every child, regardless of handicaps, should grow up. This would be good for the handicapped child, as well as for those who were not handicapped, for the former would learn to acclimate themselves to the world of the non-handicapped and the latter would learn to accept and respect others even though handicapped. Mainstreaming, as it became more popularly known, was the greatest threat of all to the stability of the classroom, and the misunderstanding of this provision was bound to affect the delivery of educational services. It would emerge as a controversy in the following two or three years and was an absolute for the handicapped interest groups who viewed any footdragging on the part of the school authorities as a serious obstacle to the success of PL 94-142. It was not a major issue in the 1977 hearings because both sides — the state and local education agencies and the handicapped interest groups — found more in the other issues to stress. Some attention was paid to it by the National Education Association which worried that if mainstreaming became the norm, local education agencies would take the opportunity to fire special education teachers because regular teachers, untrained and unwilling for the most part to teach handicapped children, would be given the teaching assignments in their regular classrooms. Special and separate education would then be considered as a frill. Hence, special education teachers would be dismissed.[24] Furthermore, mainstreamed children would either take too much time away from teaching regular children or, worse, be shunted aside in the classroom. By 1980, mainstreaming would be a paramount issue in many parts of the country.

Due Process Requirements

This is a litigious society and becoming even more so. The United States Supreme Court, beginning in the 1950's, amplified the due process clause of the 14th amendment to mean several things. Not only does the term due process mean a procedure that is due someone according to law, rules, or regulations, but it also has come to mean the kinds of procedures which are required because of the intrinsic nature of the term. Thus, to be proper, as well as due, the term has come to be rooted in certain procedural requirements such as fairness, reasonableness and the necessity for a hearing before a duly constituted legal body at certain times. If a state has a procedure according to state law that is applied in, let us say, a hearing that does not meet the scrutiny and approval of a court (either federal or state), the court might rule that the procedure is not fair, is unreasonable, or even vaguely structured. Both the federal government (there is a due process clause in the 5th Amendment

[24] *Ibid.*, 158.

that applies to the federal government) and the states now must be as certain as possible that due process is given to those who are participants in some legal procedure. One aspect of due process — the necessity for a hearing — has been written into many federal and state laws as well as in many court decisions. PL 94-142 was very specific about due process rights to be accorded to handicapped children and their parents. Section 615 (a through e) spelled out many procedural safeguards for them — examination of all records pertinent to identification, evaluation and educational placement of the handicapped child; written prior notice about contemplated changes in the policy of the local education agency; the right to have the notices in the native language of the child and parents; an impartial due process hearing for complaints with provision for appeals to an impartial review board established by the state education agency; and, the right to carry the appeal to the federal or state courts. These provisions of PL 94-142 compounded the complexities facing local school boards. Some states — like Florida, Nebraska and Rhode Island — did not provide for administrative review or such type of involved hearing procedures in their statutes, as was pointed out by the National Governors Conference. Florida and New York objected to the due process requirements in their statements before the subcommittees, and most all the witnesses testifying on behalf of the state and local education agencies as well as interest groups representing the other political bodies found the due process requirement of PL 94-142 far too complicated and out of synchronization with their state laws. They strongly believed that the requirement would result in countless cases in endless litigation. Did a school board give due process in this or that set of circumstances? Suppose a child had not been included in the hearing where the IEP was established and the parents felt that the child should have been. Was that a violation of due process great enough to go to court? The state and local education agencies saw this provision as an expensive, complicated and cumbersome way to handle the problems of educating handicapped children. They wanted to be free of the law's dictation and wanted PL-142 amended to permit each state to satisfy *its own* version of due process, not that of the federal government.

The interest groups for the handicapped, on the other hand, saw in the requirement for due process a protection against arbitrary and capricious decision-making by state and local education agencies. One after another they praised the law's mandate of procedural due process protections for handicapped children. The Childrens Defense Fund applauded the appeals system pointing out that very few states treated their handicapped impartially, the real aim of due process. The mandate of due process was "the only way to ensure that procedural safeguards are available in every state."[25] The Massachusetts Advocacy Center strongly opposed weakening due process requirements, stating that Massachusetts had even more stringent procedures than those in PL 94-142 and they worked well.[26] So, too, the Public Education Associates of New York supported the due process provisions.[27]

The interest groups for the handicapped saw due process and the role of the courts as a protector of the rights of handicapped children and the agencies saw them as a threat to their governance.

The Position of the Carter Administration

The Administration did not testify at the Senate Subcommittee hearings in June, but in September, Ernest Boyer, Commissioner of Education and Edwin Martin, Deputy Commissioner of Education and head of the Bureau of Edu-

[25] *Ibid.*, 84.
[26] Senate Subcommittee Hearings, 240.
[27] 213-216.

cation for the Handicapped, appeared before the House Subcommittee on Select Education to summarize what the BEH had done thus far to ensure compliance of the states with PL 94-142. Not only had the BEH prepared the regulations in a thorough and painstaking manner, it had also approved all state and territory plans submitted by 1977 and had received all plans but those from one State (New Mexico) for 1978. Furthermore, the BEH was monitoring state progress in the implementation of the plans and had visited half the states and 100 local school districts to ensure their plans fell in line with legislative and program expectation. The remaining 25 states would be visited within a short time. Consultation with interest groups would continue even though the writing of the regulations was finished in order to maintain communication with them and be responsive to them as well.

Commissioner Boyer took issue with the states' objections, as we have outlined above, by claiming that the conflicts they saw with their own laws and constitutions did not seem to be real and, if troublesome, could be administratively modified. They should not be resolved by amending PL 94-142 at this time, and he underscored the BEH's assurance, in particular, that the Individualized Education Program "was not to be construed as a contract in which certain predictable outcomes were to be expected or for which the school might be held accountable." It was only an "arrangement to provide" services to a handicapped child. All things considered, he said, this was "not the time to introduce additional amendments.[28]

In his attempt to clarify the federal role in educating handicapped children, Boyer said it was to give "some sense of equity and design and clarity to an obligation that has been inherently rooted in the public education system all along; enriched. . .by some federal funds, recognizing that it

[28] *Ibid.*, 96–98.

is an enormously serious obligation."[29] When asked to clarify the relationship of Section 504 of the Rehabilitation Act of 1973 to the mandate of PL 94-142 that every child was to be guaranteed a "free appropriate public education," Commissioner Boyer said that under the civil rights mandate of Section 504 (enforced by the Office of Civil Rights) no institution receiving federal funds could discriminate against the handicapped and indeed the requirement of a state to deliver a "free appropriate public education" to handicapped children — if it participated in the federal assistance program under PL 94-142 — could converge with Section 504. As Commissioner Martin also pointed out, a state was free to participate in PL 94-142's program or not. All but one were so far. The Education for All Handicapped Children Act simply helped the states to carry out what was their Constitutional obligations (under the 14th Amendment) and statutory obligations under Section 504.

The extent of the mandatory nature of Section 504 was dealt with in the Supreme Court decision of *Southeastern Community College v. Davis*, decided on June 11, 1979. The issue in the case was whether a partially deaf woman licensed as a practical nurse by the State of North Carolina in 1967 could be refused admission to that part of a college's registered nurse program which required contacts with patients. Southeastern Community College received some federal funds and therefore was required to observe the mandate of Section 504 that "no otherwise qualified handicapped individual" could be discriminated against "under any program or activity receiving Federal financial assistance." In 1974 the college rejected her admission on the grounds that clinical training and safe participation in a program which required full physical skills and dexterity did not violate Section 504 in that the applicant, because of her particular handicap, was not "otherwise qualified," even though she was profi-

[29] *Ibid.*, 102.

cient at lip-reading. Frances B. Davis, who could not thereby be licensed by North Carolina as a registered nurse, brought suit in Federal District Court in North Carolina charging that her denial of admission was based solely on her handicap and therefore violated Section 504. The Court found for the college, but on appeal, the Court of Appeals for the Fourth Circuit reversed that decision. The United States Supreme Court then accepted the case on appeal by the State of North Carolina. On June 11, 1979, the Supreme Court unanimously ruled for the college saying that the Rehabilitation Act of 1973 and its Section 504 does not require a college either to accept someone whose handicap prevents him or her from meeting the requirements of a particular program or to provide "extensive modifications" that would make the student's participation physically possible. Of course, wrote Associate Justice Lewis F. Powell, Jr., speaking for the unanimous Court, the physical qualifications for the program had to be "legitimate." In this instance, the ability of a registered nurse "to understand speech without reliance on lip reading is necessary for patient safety." The intent of Section 504 is not "to impose an affirmative action obligation on all recipients of Federal funds" nor does it require "an educational institution to lower or to affect substantial modifications of standards to accommodate a handicapped person."

The authors can only speculate about this Supreme Court decision's impact on PL 94-142. In our opinion, the decision was based on what was an "appropriate" education for someone to have in order to become licensed as a registered nurse. The extent of the "appropriateness" of the education can be determined by the educational institution offering services — this instance, the Southeastern Community College. PL 94-142's mandate that every handicapped child is entitled to a free appropriate public education is in the context of the *Southeastern Community College v. Davis* decision in that the law states that a handicapped child must have that which is "appropriate." The educational and related services that the school must deliver is related to the extent of the handicap of the child. Thus the school is obligated to deliver that which is "appropriate" to the child's condition. The Individualized Education Program (IEP) is designed by the education agency, with participation in the process by the parents and the child, *where appropriate.* Certainly, the court can become involved in a suit brought by parents who might be dissatisfied with the decision made by the education agency as incorporated in the child's IEP. But due process safeguards for the child are written in PL 94-142 and the regulations. The court would have to rule, in such a suit, whether or not the degree of "appropriateness" was reasonable, given the extent of the child's handicap. This in essence is the principle laid down by the Supreme Court in the Southeastern Community College case. Thus, we think, the decision does not impede, hinder or make unconstitutional PL 94-142. Nor does the decision lessen the obligations of the State and local education agencies to guarantee every handicapped child a "free appropriate public education." It actually substantiates the intent of PL 94-142.

The Carter Administration position on PL 94-142, that the Congress should support the implementation of the law as it stood, was supported by the interest groups for the handicapped. The American Friends Service Committee did not put much stock in the concerns expressed by the deliverers of educational and related services. "It is not unusual for state and local education agencies," said its spokeswoman, "initially to see laws which extend human and educational rights and opportunities as administrative nightmares which will result in unresolvable dilemmas and traumatic departures from past practices. . .Yet, once these laws begin to fall into place administrators learn that they can work with the law, they can serve the beneficiaries of the law. ."[30] Congress should lend its support to the BEH's efforts to see to it that the States' "annual plans meet the requirements for planning and counting" and that due process, the Individualized Education Program and "mainstreaming" requirements be enforced by the BEH.[31]

The Council for Exceptional Children argued that when all is said and done PL 94-142 requires little the courts and many states have not already required and places no unique financial burden on the states.[32] The American Coalition of Citizens with Disabilities wanted no tampering with PL 94-142 and hoped that the federal government would enforce the law strictly and without a permissiveness towards the state and local education agencies that would permit the misspending of federal funds.[33] The Bureau of Education for the Handicapped cannot be forceful enough in administering the law, argued the Childrens Defense Fund. The problems in implementing PL 94-142 merely "stem from an old-fashioned resistance to change by a small number of States and school districts. They stem from a lingering unwillingness to recognize that handicapped children have a right to an education and to sufficient state and local financial support for this education."[34]

The Subcommittees' Position

John Brademas, chairman of the House Subcommittee on Select Education, sympathetically sided with the interest groups for the handicapped, chiding the states for their complaints even before PL 94-142 was to go into full effect. Addressing the representative of the National Association of

[30] Senate Subcommittee Hearings, 177.

[31] *Ibid.*, 178.

[32] House Subcommittee Hearings, 61.

[33] *Ibid.*, 77.

[34] *Ibid.*, 81.

State Boards of Education (NASBE), Brademas said that he was struck by a certain anomaly in his mind:

> . . .it was almost entirely as a consequence of enactments by State legislatures and by rulings of State courts holding that handicapped children have a constitutional right to an education appropriate to their needs that Congress responded. You are the ones that started all this. We didn't. Pennsylvania is the place where most of it began. It is a little mystifying to me, now that we have tried to respond to your argument that it costs a lot of money to educate handicapped children, and now that we have tried to give you some funds with which to help you meet that burden that we both acknowledge, that you don't seem very happy about it.[35]

Brademas pointed out that the Council for Exceptional Children had effectively countered every complaint by the states and local education agencies. He was seconded in his defense of PL 94-142 by Minnesota Congressman Albert H. Quie, the ranking Republican on the House Education and Labor Committee and who often sat with the House Subcommittee on Select Education as an *ex officio* member.[36]

It was apparent from the questions asked and statements made by all the members of the Senate Subcommittee on the Handicapped, chaired by Senator Jennings Randolph of West Virginia, that they too were dedicated to seeing that PL 94-142 was fully implemented. After all, both subcommittees were the ones responsible for writing the concept of a "free appropriate public education" for handicapped children and all that went with it into Federal law. They wanted to see it work and did not feel the arguments of the states worth their concern.

By the end of 1977, after the last set of hearings, several aspects had emerged.

[35] *Ibid.*, 37.
[36] *Ibid.*, 39–40.

1. Support of the aims of PL 94-142 in Congress was on a non-partisan basis.
2. The Carter Administration, at the time, was committed to enforcing the law and doing everything reasonably possible to have the states comply with its provisions.
3. State and local education agencies were pessimistic about the effectiveness of the law and their ability to make it work unless there were massive infusions of even more federal funds than the Congress felt necessary.
4. Interest groups for the handicapped were determined to continue to pressure Congress to support the law and now found that they had also to confront State and local education agencies' resistance to full implementation. They also realized that they would have rising opposition from some teachers and their organizations that feared the implications for them in the "mainstreaming" requirements of the law.

The next two years saw PL 94-142 continue to grow in importance as interest groups for the handicapped, state and local education agencies and small groups representing parents in the localities broadened their publications and reached out to parents of handicapped children to make them aware of what they and their children were entitled to under PL 94-142.

7

Does PL 94-142 Work?

Anyone who has followed the long process involved in the creation of PL 94-142 and its implementation in the first year or two after the writing of the rules and regulations, can be expected to ask — Does it work? The answer, like the law itself, is necessarily complex. PL 94-142's efficacy for solving the plight of undereducated handicapped children depends in great measure on the good will of the deliverers of educational and related services to handicapped children and the availability of both federal and state funds to pay for those services. Because the political process in any issue never ends, the answer is in the eye of the beholder, depending on whose viewpoint is being sought. Those who seek the answer must come first to a full understanding of the intent of PL 94-142.

Congress' basic intent in enacting PL 94-142 was to assure the statutory right of every handicapped child to a free appropriate public education. The law established many specific guidelines for the states which opted to take part in the program and authorized funds for several fiscal years. But authorization of funds in the original law is not appropriation of funds, which come from Congress only in response to the request of the President as exemplified in his annual budget presented to the Congress. And, the appropriations of federal funds for the states to carry out their responsibilities under the law have in no way met the ceilings established by PL 94-142. We shall go into this problem in later detail. Guidelines too are just that — only guidelines, subject to interpretation by the various state and local education agencies as well as the federal government. A state may believe itself to be in compliance with the law, but the Bureau of Education for the Handicapped may well believe the state falls short of such compliance. The political process related to the principles and practices of federalism then comes into play as the federal and state governments vie back and forth to come to a meeting of minds. Parents of a handicapped child, too, might well feel that the Individualized Education Program devised by local education authorities does not fully meet the needs of their child and therefore seek redress according to the rules of due process as established by PL 94-142 and the rules and regulations written by the BEH. The office of Civil Rights is authorized by law to look into complaints of discrimination of the handicapped. The OCR claimed in 1979 that almost all the complaints had been resolved. We could go on pointing out the many things that can happen, and go wrong, after the bill has been passed and the "regs" written, but the point has been well made. The enactment of a law does not end the process. The process goes on and is newly directed and shaped by events, practices, and new interpretations.

PL 94-142's intent to assure every handicapped child a free appropriate public education was strengthened by Section 504 of the Rehabilitation Act, which states flatly that no entity receiving federal funds can legally discriminate against a person because of that person's handicap. The handicapped child *is* such a person and also has a constitutional, as well as statutory, right to be treated equally with the nonhandicapped. PL 94-142, Section 504, and the equal protection of the laws clause of the 14th amendment give handicapped children and those who represent them in the political arena a permanent, irrevocable hunting license, so to speak, to seek the best ways to have the intent of Congress carried out and to secure federal and state funds with which to do it.

The political process, then, becomes more, not less complicated. A bill becomes a law and regulations, subject to interpretation and possibly litigation, are then written. Implementing and enforcing the law, which by virtue of its passage by the Congress becomes an output of public policy, creates a new relationship between the states and the federal government. The public policy output fashions a brand new set of circumstances that in turn feed back to the entities that had input into the political process out of which emerged the law in the first place. In the case of PL 94–142, the handicapped interest groups, state and local education agencies, and various other groups in the education community had to deal with a new process — carrying out the intent of the law, examining the extent of compliance on the part of the states and local education agencies with the law, and suggesting ways to improve the delivery of education and related services. To complicate the matter further, each state has its own specific way of dealing with the issue of educating handicapped children which must now be blended with or made subordinate or supplementary to the federal law. Fifty different sets of state standards exist. PL 94–142 is an attempt to make the concept of a free appropriate public education for all handicapped children a national norm.

But what is appropriate? Must the education offered be appropriate within the context of a handicapped child's ability to learn given the nature of the handicapped? Or, does the handicapped child have to have a handicap which is appropriate to the education and related services being offered? How do you fairly measure the degree of appropriateness in the first place? Does the government's responsibility end with the end of the school year and begin again

with the beginning of the next school year? Does a handicapped child have more difficulty than the non-handicapped
in retention of that which has just been learned and, accordingly, should be treated differently during the summer
months than others? These and many more questions are
raised because of the passage of PL 94-142 and become part
of a new political process. Thus the law and its policy output
feed back to the sources of the law. Only the process itself
can answer the original question —does it work? Once again
we have to look at the components which relate to one
another in the process.

It is too early to tell just how successful PL 94-142 has
been in bringing a free appropriate public education to all
handicapped children. We can, however, look to the components in the early 1980's in our study of PL 94-142 and at
least speculate on the prospects for the future. We shall,
therefore, briefly examine the view from 1) the Bureau of
Education for the Handicapped, the agency empowered
to oversee compliance with the law, 2) the state and local
education agencies charged with carrying out the intent of
Congress, 3) the handicapped interest groups, the prodders
and watchdogs, and 4) the Congress which appropriates the
federal funds to pay for the federal commitment.

The View from the Bureau of Education For the Handicapped

Like any other federal bureaucracy, the Bureau of Education for the Handicapped is concerned with its own interest
and image. It must justify its existence by presenting to
Congress its past record in as favorable a light as possible,
thereby properly legitimizing its search for more funds and
authority. Unless an agency can satisfactorily show it has
used its statutory authority with prudence, judiciousness,
objectivity and fairness, has expended federal funds with

care, and has acted in accordance with the intent of Congress, it becomes fair game for Congressional and other critics. The BEH, accordingly, likes to thrust its best foot forward and argue that the assurance of a free appropriate public education for every handicapped child in the nation has proceeded apace and will continue to do so under its thoughtful guidance.

BEH records will show that it willingly serves as an information source for local education agencies, state departments of education and concerned parents, for example: Informing a local education agency it has to pay transportation costs of a handicapped child as a related service incidental to the handicap; telling a state department of education that it *must* withhold PL 94-142 funds from a local school district which cannot satisfactorily demonstrate it is meeting state and federal requirements for the education of handicapped children in its district; and, stating to a parent of a handicapped child that although the child's Individualized Education Program (IEP) is not a contract guaranteeing the parent that the child will achieve the growth projected in the IEP, the parent retains the right to involve due process procedures if the parent feels the agency and teachers have not made good faith efforts to bring the child's level of achievement to the projected goals of the plan.[1]

In January, 1979, the BEH issued a report to Congress on the progress that had been made toward securing a free appropriate public education for handicapped children.[2] The Bureau had conducted many surveys in several states and had commissioned at least two contract studies to determine how PL 94-142 was being implemented in the states. The Bureau reported that progress was being made and that the states

[1] T. B. Irvin (BEH) to K. A. Stormer (HEW: re; Orange County of California) 2 April, 1979; W. D. Tyrell (BEH) to B. Weithers (Kansas) 14 March 1979; T. B. Irvin (BEH) to J. C. Pheil (Georgia) 19 June 1979.

[2] *Progress Toward a Free Appropriate Public Education, a Report to Congress on the Implementation of Public Law 94-142*, U.S. Department of Health, Education and Welfare, January, 1979.

were indeed committed to provide all handicapped children with a free appropriate public education. The law had not been in effect for very long and naturally, it was still too early for all states to be complying *fully* with the intent of PL 94-142. The Bureau primarily emphasized the elusiveness of an accurate count of all handicapped children in the nation. Each state was responsible for identifying and counting its handicapped children, and accuracy of the state counts could not be depended upon. Census statistics and widespread surveys used by the BEH to determine (or guess) the total number of handicapped children in the nation had led the Bureau to believe that about 12 per cent of all school-age children had some sort of handicap covered by PL 94-142. Until all identified handicapped children were being properly served, the Bureau could opt for more funds and authority, thus building its own agency into a more and more important entity. But the count by the states showed that only about 7 per cent of all school-age children were handicapped. The BEH statistics showed that 3.681 million handicapped children were served in the 1977-78 school year, 3.72 million in 1978-79, an estimated 3.8 million in 1979-80, with a BEH goal of 3.9 million in 1980-81. About half, therefore, of the counted handicapped children were being served. But the BEH thought there were many more who had been left out of the count, and the BEH was troubled by the considerable variation in the per cent of the school-age population served as handicapped.

Understandably, then, the BEH wanted to increase the number of handicapped children served by more careful monitoring of state identification and counting procedures and by seeking support of public and private agencies to identify the unserved. The BEH's major immediate objective was to identify, evaluate, and place all handicapped children in a proper educational setting. The BEH had examined 26 states between November, 1976 and May, 1977 to determine how the "least restrictive environment" or "mainstreaming" provisions of PL 94-142 were being implemented. "Main-streaming" was meeting with resistance from some teachers and parents of non-handicapped children, and 15 of the 26 States had not yet adopted placement policies which met the requirements of the federal law. Nevertheless, the BEH believed the prognosis was good and that state and local education agencies were sincerely attempting to apply the principle. But the BEH concluded that federal monitoring: (which meant by the BEH) would *always* be necessary to ensure compliance of the states with PL 94-142. In summary, the BEH report observed that activity at the federal, state and local levels in the first year of PL 94-142's implementation had been impressive, commitment to the goals of the Act was widespread and genuine, administrative and logistical problems expected to impede implementation were being resolved, but states would have to exert greater effort toward finding undiagnosed handicapped children already in school.

In his testimony to the House Subcommittee on Select Education, conducting oversight hearings on PL 94-142 late in 1979, Edwin W. Martin, Deputy Commissioner of Education and head of the BEH, stressed that despite frustration and imperfections, there had been a definite and fundamental improvement of the educational system for handicapped children. Ninety per cent of the states showed increases in children served in 1978-79, and states were developing more interagency cooperation among those delivering mental health, education and social services. Making certain that the House Subcommittee could easily see that the BEH was doing a fine job, Martin, who became Assistant Secretary of Education for Special Education and Rehabilitative Services in 1980 under the reorganization of the new Department of Education, quoted from a study by the Education Turnkey Systems, Inc., done under commission from the BEH, and completed in May, 1979:

In all sites, major activities were initiated in response to the Federal mandate: indeed, never have so many local and state agencies done so much with so few Federal dollars to implement a Federal education mandate.[3]

The View from the State and Local Education Agencies

State and local public officials are innately suspicious of federal agencies. Washington is looked upon as a far-removed entity which can never fully understand the complexities of local problems. Even when the federal government responds to the needs of the states with some kind of legislative remedy, the states and localities seem to remain unappreciative of Federal efforts. Furthermore, when the federal government tries to establish some sort of uniform system throughout the nation, whether it be a criminal code, an interstate highway system or an educational norm, it is bound to have only limited success. The reason for this is rooted in very nature of federalism. The relationship between the nation and the states is not neat and clean. The federal government, for example, administers federal law through federal regions, which encompass several states as a basic unit. One regional interpretation of some federal rule or regulation might well be different from that of another, and the difference may continue to exist *ad infinitum*. Even in an interpretation of the Constitution, one Circuit Court of Appeals may rule one way in some case before it, and another Circuit Court may rule in another way in a case that has a similar set of circumstances. Both courts base their rulings on the same section and language of the U.S. Constitution, but unless one or the other case is later ruled on by the U.S. Supreme Court, both rulings, different though they may be, will be in effect in their respective judicial jurisdictions. We could go on with many examples of variations

[3] See also, Executive Summary, Contract NO. 300-77-0528, *Case Study* of the Implementation of PL 94-142, Education Turnkey Systems, Inc., May 31, 1979, p. 1.

among the states because of the federal principle, where the federal government shares some authority with the states (concurrent jurisdiction), is inferior to the states which have residual powers in some areas (although this seems to be shrinking rapidly), and is supreme over the states under the national supremacy clause of the Constitution. Federalism is not a neatly defined concept. Rather than the three-layered cake of federal, state and local jurisdictions wherein each governmental entity is certain of its own role, and each role is clearly differentiated, federalism, as the late Morton Grodzins has pointed out, is more like a marble cake of three flavors, swirling and blending in different sized eddies. Education law in the United States is a fine example of the marble cake theory of Grodzins. The Bureau of Education for the Handicapped, now under the Office of Special Education and Rehabilitative Services of the new Department of Education, fashions itself the superior governmental body or agency which is required to bring the states and localities into compliance with PL 94-142. Its report on the implementation of the law is necessarily colored by its own view of its statutory authority to carry out the intent of the law − to see to it that the states and local education agencies deliver a free appropriate public education to every handicapped child in the nation. A federal agency has the bias of the top layer of a three layer cake. State and local officials, however, tend to view the political process inherent in federalism more along the lines of Grodzins' marble cake theory, taking refuge in the real differences among the States which cannot be blended into national uniformity. The States are different in size, population, wealth, resources and laws related to home rule concepts. Local officials, too, realize that the localities within a given state are also different from one another and it is very difficult indeed to invoke a state-wide edict on basically different localities. Elementary and secondary education has traditionally been the responsibility of local government, as derived from state constitutional and legislative authority. Deep-rooted traditions are hard to change, and the field of education is a national mosaic. Imposition of a national set of standards in education is almost impossible.

When Congress wrote PL 94-142, it hoped that handicapped children would now receive their due, but Congress never did define, nor could it, what *exactly* was due them. Congress took refuge, as it often does, in the ambiguity of the word "appropriate" when it expressed in an Act of Congress what was due handicapped children, a free appropriate public education. Free means — no cost to the children or their parents. Public means — the same education for handicapped children that other children receive in the public schools. Both those definitions are, it seems to us, self-evident. The meaning of "appropriate" is not self-evident and must be defined and redefined in case after case. To state and local education agencies, therefore, the implementation of PL 94-142 could not be as cavalierly treated as the BEH had done in its overview and evaluation. State and local education agencies were not as cheerful as the Bureau in their view of implementation of PL 94-142. Wary of Federal encroachment on their traditional prerogatives of determining the education system of their states and localities, even though they had gingerly supported Federal assistance in the formulation of PL 94-142, the SEA's and LEA's looked upon Federal attempts to bring them into compliance with PL 94-142 as overly excessive. What did a bureaucracy in Washington know about the real difficulties of coping with handicapped children or complying with such a detailed list of rules and regulations as outlined in the *Federal Register*? Not that the SEA's and LEA's were defying the law. They were committed to it, but implementation of the law was not as simple as the BEH made it out to be. They saw the problems of compliance centering on the following.

1. Not Enough Federal Funds to Begin With. The costs of

educating a handicapped child had always been at least double that of educating a non-handicapped child. In fact, the costs of educating handicapped children were increasing at a faster rate than those of educating non-handicapped children. Most people were not anxious to increase state and local taxes for any reason, and demands for tax relief among many were vocal and strident. The gap between the costs of educating handicapped and non-handicapped children was therefore widening, and neither the state nor local districts could go on much longer without massive federal funds (naturally, the states and localities would prefer a bare minimum of federal regulation). Another, unexpected high cost of educating handicapped children was running ahead at a rapidly increasing rate. PL 94–142 required that when a child's handicap was of such nature that the public school could not carry out its mandate, the child had to be placed by the public agency within the jurisdiction of a suitable private institution, free of costs to the parents. In other words, if a public school could not handle the education of a handicapped child because of the extent of the handicap or because of the inadequate facilities of the public school, the child had to be placed in a private school with the state and/or local school district charged with paying the full costs of education and all related services (which might include room, board, transportation as well as tuition). These costs were extremely high and several states found themselves severely strapped for funds. They wanted either federal relief specifically for these kinds of costs or release from PL 94–142's requirement to educate all handicapped children equally. Did not the word "appropriate" mean "where possible?" And, if not possible for an SEA or LEA to educate certain handicapped children, should not that end the matter unless the federal government took over complete financial responsibility? So thought many of the states. The federal law required them to provide more services than they could possibly afford, and although they were committed to carry out the intent of the law, they believed they were unable to deliver comprehensive services to all handicapped children, in public or private schools.

2. *The Teacher Problem.* There was more than one aspect involved in this issue. First, there was a continual shortage of special education teachers. Second, there was a problem of balancing off the role of the regular teacher in a regular classroom in which a handicapped child had been placed between dealing with the handicapped child properly and not taking too much time away from the non-handicapped children. The strain on the regular teachers was real, and teachers' unions began to take a dim view of these new responsibilities in the light of teachers' demands for more money and better working conditions. Third, teachers were required to spend an inordinate amount of time developing, carrying out and evaluating a handicapped child's Individualized Education Program. Every time a handicapped child moved to a different jurisdiction, the IEP had to be done over again, and in any case the IEP had to be updated at regular intervals. Teachers were becoming clerks and bureaucrats, and many of them resented it.

3. *Too Much Paperwork.* The ever increasing paperwork was a constant complaint of SEA's, LEA's, school administrators and teachers. An over-reliance on details, the need to dot every *i* and cross every *t* and the requirement to adhere to strict concepts of due process (often not clearly understood) were simply too much for them to handle, particularly given the fact that no extra remuneration was in the offing.

4. *The Opposition of Parents of the Non-Handicapped.* Now that handicapped children had come into their legal rights, they were more visible in the community and the classroom. But many parents of non-handicapped children

viewed with alarm the alleged disruption of the educational system by the Least Restrictive Environment requirement. *Their* children were now receiving less attention than previously, and they felt they were being short-changed. Handicapped children had rights, to be sure, but so did their non-handicapped children. Thus there was a noticeable development of a tendency of a serious split between parents of handicapped and non-handicapped children. (This split was not unlike that which had developed between parents divided on the issue of busing to alleviate racial discrimination in the public schools.)

5. The Complaints about the BEH. Whereas the BEH looked upon itself as the Federal Agency charged with bringing about State and Local compliance with PL 94-142, the SEA's and LEA's wanted the BEH to be more of a support group and less of a compliance agency. Federal agencies are supposed to enforce the law, and of course the 180 or so people in the BEH should see to it that "laws are faithfully executed" as they are indirectly charged by the U.S. Constitution as arms of the executive authority of the President. But in the field of education, probably more so than in other areas, those who administer and teach do not look upon themselves as agents of government but rather as professionals dedicated to their work. They therefore want aid and guidance from the Federal government, when they feel in need, not orders and directives. Just because they receive federal funds, they usually believe, does not legitimize federal control. And, control is what the BEH represented to them.

One thing can be inferred from the view of the SEA's and LEA's, however. PL 94-142 is here to stay. None of the major state and local interest groups—(like the national Association of State Directors of Special Education (NASDSE), Council of Chief State Officers (CCSSO), or the National School Boards Association (NSBA) — whose representatives testified before the House Subcommittee on Select

Education in September and October, 1979 and the Senate Subcommittee on the Handicapped in July and October, 1979 asked for repeal of the law. They all supported the intent of the law and congratulated Congress for its fine work in enacting the legislation. It was pointed out by NASDSE that most of the States had indeed changed their laws to bring them in line with PL 94-142's approach to educating handicapped children. There was no turning back. The system had only to be more finely tuned, and with more federal money and more federal understanding, patience and forbearance, the intent of PL 94-142 would eventually be fully met.

The View from the Interest Groups for Handicapped Children

The major interest groups which had fought for Federal legislation to enhance the lives of handicapped children by providing for a free appropriate public education with PL 94-142 continued to press on after passage of the law. They are the strongest, most organized support for handicapped children, willing to push the Congress to legislate even more federal aid and the state and local education agencies to comply with the law. The education interest groups which represent state and local government (such as the National Association of State Directors of Special Education, the National School Boards Association, the Council of Chief State School Officers etc.) have any number of broad constituencies to whom they are responsible and which vary in scope. The education of handicapped children is only one of many education interests for which they use state supported funds (and Federal grants) to lobby the Congress and the Executive Branch in Washington. Along with NASDSE, NSBA and the CCSSO, other groups such as the National Conference of State Legislatures, the National Governors'

Association, the National Association of Counties, and the National Association of Secondary School Principals use their influence wherever they can not only in Washington but also in their state capitals. They usually take the side of state and local government against federal encroachment on their prerogatives and against the demands made on state and local governments by such organized labor groups as the National Education Association and the American Federation of Teachers. The latter two groups, for example, have a great deal more to be concerned about than educating handicapped children. They lobby for higher salaries for teachers, better working conditions, and a better shake for teachers in general against elected and administrative school officials. Teacher groups have not been in the forefront in the fight to assure a proper education for handicapped children, although of course teachers of special education do have an abiding concern for such a concept. Their priorities lean towards what they consider to be broader issues of education policy. Naturally, enough, the interest groups which represent handicapped children find themselves in an adversary relationship with the state and local education interest groups as well as most teacher associations.

The Council for Exceptional Children, the National Association for Retarded Citizens, the Children's Defense Fund and the countless splinter groups representing children with impaired hearing, sight and specific emotional disorders as well as those who are orthopedically impaired seek ways of improving the lot of one specific group in society — handicapped children. They are very much aware of the subtle resistance to increasing the general welfare for handicapped children emanating from tax-reduction groups, fearful parents of non-handicapped children and teachers unable or unwilling to take that extra step to help handicapped children. Too, there is enough evidence of state and local resistance to allocating financial resources necessary for the education of handicapped children so that, despite some increase of expenditures at the state and local level, the interest groups for handicapped children continue to press for more financial, moral and legal commitment by state and local authorities.

Throughout the nation, particularly in the wealthier and more populated states, there are a number of small groups and wealthy parents who, with the backing of the traditional interest groups for handicapped children, seek a redress of their grievances in the courts to advance the cause of handicapped children. Dockets at both federal and state levels are getting heavier with parental claims. At the federal level, parents can invoke the many facets of PL 94-142, and at the state level there is some state law and even the Constitution to cite. We shall refer to just two recent cases as examples of litigation wherein parents are joined by interest groups in bringing suit against state and local education agencies.

ARMSTRONG V. KLINE (JUNE 21, 1979)

Five severely handicapped students and their parents filed a class action suit in the U.S. District Court for the Eastern District of Pennsylvania against Pennsylvania and Philadelphia school officials charging that the state and local educational agency violated PL 94-142 and the 14th amendment's equal protection of the laws and due process clauses by failing to provide special education for the children during the summer months between the 180-day school years. The plaintiffs argued that Pennsylvania's policy of restricting education and related services to the 180-day school year deprived the handicapped children of an "appropriate" education under the requirements of PL 94-142. The Judge in the case agreed and interpreted the Federal law to mean that the state had to continue the education program through the summer months because the summer interruption without such a program resulted in a loss of hard-won skills learned in the regular school year. He accordingly ordered the school district and the state to establish summer programs because, in his view, PL 94–142's intent could only be carried out by a full year's program. (PL 94–142 made no reference to this issue at all.) The plaintiffs were represented by attorney's from the Education Law Center. Pennsylvania and Philadelphia thereupon appealed the District Court Judge's decision to the 3rd U.S. Circuit Court of Appeals. The National School Boards Association and the State of Maine then filed friend-of-the-court briefs (*Amicus Curiae*) to oppose the mandatory summer programs for handicapped children ruled by the District Judge. Taking issue with the parents of the handicapped children, NSBA and the State of Maine claimed that if the decision were upheld it would have a "substantial effect on the content, financing and administration of the education program of every school district in the country," and the increased costs of such a program would be inconsistent with fiscal and administrative responsibilities of the States. Interest groups for handicapped children, like the National Center for Law and the Handicapped, are of course very concerned with the final disposition of this case, and they oppose in general the view of NSBA and the state agencies.

THE JOSÉ P. V. ARMBACH CASE (DECEMBER 14, 1979)

A group of handicapped children and their parents, represented by the Brooklyn Legal Services Corporation B; the Handicapped Persons Legal Support Unit, and the Community Action for Legal Services and supported by the Public Education Association and the Advocates for Children of New York brought suit against the City of New York claiming their children were being deprived of an appropriate public education because the city had not placed the children nor properly identified them. The Federal District Judge in Brooklyn handed down a 45-page judgment ordering the City of New York and its Board of Education to act within 60 days to evaluate and place handicapped children in "appropriate" programs. The judge ordered an immediate census of all handicapped children under 21 years of age, the establishment of an "outreach office" by the city to disseminate information about handicapped children's programs, and the provision by the city of a "full continuum of educational programs and services," including bilingual efforts for students with "limited English proficiency" as well as sufficient "alternative day-school center programs" and "residential programs" for students requiring them. The judge's far-reaching orders were *his* interpretations of the meaning of the word "appropriate" in the language of PL 94-142. The City of New York decided not to appeal the decision but to try to carry out the judge's orders which were estimated to cost an extra $350 million.

These two cases are cited here to emphasize that without the creation of organized interest groups to advance the cause of handicapped children, without their continued interest in seeing to it that handicapped children get their full due under federal and state law, and without the involvement of the courts within the political process, there can be no real hope for handicapped children to receive a free, appropriate public education and all related services.

The political process of a pluralistic society requires constant watchfulness by all groups and factions and their commitment to achieve their goals within the context of a democratic society.

The View from the Congress: How Much is Enough?

For an idea to become a law and be implemented effectively by some executive agency, Congress must supply two things: legislative authority and funds.

The plight of handicapped children was quickly understood by Congress in the 1960's as their interest groups dramatically laid out their needs in open hearings of the Subcommittees charged with jurisdiction over handicapped legislation. Congress turned its legislative ear to handicapped children and their representatives who argued forcefully for the equal right of handicapped children to a free appropriate public education. Congressional response was gradual, however. The federal government was given statutory authority to do something, but at first not much, for the education of handicapped children. Congress, after all, represents political and geographic constituencies which traditionally have retained control over public and private education policies. Early Congressional legislation to alleviate the distress of handicapped children was directed at helping States cope with the financial problems posed in the education of handicapped children. Congress did not seek to invoke the heavy hand of federal regulation on the States and local school districts by mandating forthwith the delivery of education and related services to handicapped children. State and local resistance to this approach, if the attempt had been made to force it on the states and local school agencies immediately, would have been strong. In the 1960's, state and local school agencies merely encouraged the Congress to lend a financial hand but did not ask for passage of statutory mandates. The mandate that every state and local education agency deliver a free appropriate public education to all handicapped children, as outlined in PL 94-142, more or less sneaked up on them, as the interest groups for the handicapped looked for their victories one at a time: some federal funds, establishment of the Bureau of Education for the Handicapped, writing into federal law language which could be used to pressure state and local education agencies to deliver services, the permanent rooting of the BEH, strengthening the delivery services by the Federal use of the expression "free appropriate public education," more legislative language spelling out procedural safeguards for handicapped children and their parents, more and more federal funds, and finally helping in the long but eventually successful fight on the part of most of the education community to establish a separate Department of Education, which was enacted into law in 1979 with the agreement of President Carter.

The Congress, through the Committees and Subcommittees which have jurisdiction over handicapped legislation, never opposed the interest groups for handicapped children. Interest groups had friends in the other two anchors of the "iron triangle": the Committee and Subcommittee staffs and the BEH staffers, all of whom were committed to advance the cause of handicapped children. The various oversight hearings held through the years gave the interest groups a chance to bring Congress up to date on progress made for handicapped children and to place on the public record their achievements in pressing state and local education agencies to devote more of their efforts to deliver needed services. Congress responded through the years by gradually strengthening the foothold in the executive branch that the interest groups wanted. The end result was the establishment of an agency that spoke not only for the executive branch but also the handicapped themselves. Congress looked hard in 1979 at what it had created and decided that it was indeed good. Handicapped children now had the statutory right to a free appropriate public education that their spokespersons had fought for in the lobbies of Congress.

But the Congressional supply of funds was another matter. In the development of legislation that led to PL 94-142, Congress had played an almost single-handed role. To be sure, the Kennedy and Johnson Administrations had been supportive, but the Nixon and Ford Administrations had not been, and PL 94-142 had been developed and enacted during the latters' period in office. Legislation for handicapped children is not something easily opposed by anyone. President Ford had "reluctantly" signed the measure into law, for a veto would have been quickly overriden. During the four years of Carter's Administration, PL 94–142 became more firmly rooted and accepted by the Administration and indeed by state and local education agencies. Congress could look upon PL 94–142 with great satisfaction. But a law that establishes the legal authority of an executive agency and authorizes a ceiling of expenditures for future fiscal years, cannot guarantee that future Congresses will in fact appropriate all the money authorized by it.

Once a bill becomes a law, the appropriations process for supplying Federal funds is entirely different from that in developing the original enabling legislation. The most important factor in appropriations is the budget process itself. The budget that is presented to the Congress each year by the President is huge and all-encompassing. It is the sum total of all the requests made by the departments and agencies of the entire federal government, as sifted and synthesized by the Office of Management and Budget, a key agency in the Executive Office of the President. The OMB takes all these requests which have been previously funnelled through intra-Departmental and intra-Agency entities and works them into some sort of legislative-fiscal sense for the President. The President's annual budget is related to his then current legislative program for the Congress. All departments and agencies are subject to the President's priorities, as he sees them at the time. A particular President might want to spend more money on military hardware and less on other things etc. He is not bound by the expenditures authorized in any legislation to seek full funding from the Congress. In fact, he too is under the constraints of pressures generated by countless interest groups, Congressional leaders, and the prevailing economic conditions, not to mention the state of international affairs.

After the enactment of PL 94–142, the handicapped constituencies, therefore, had a problem in bringing their budgetary requests to the top of the President's list of priorities. Not only did the BEH, interest groups for the handicapped, and a few staffers have to settle for lower-priority status because of other programs that had to be funded, but they also suffered because until 1980 "Education" was only one part of the very large Department of Health, Education and Welfare. Health and Welfare have much bigger national constituencies than does Education. And, the education for the handicapped constituency is relatively small in comparison with other education constituencies — those in the elementary, secondary and higher education fields in general. During the early years of implementation and federal funding of PL 94-142, therefore, the handicapped constituency had to share its financial requests with other, more powerful spokespersons of other education constituencies. It had taken ten years to enact PL 94-142, and surely the handicapped constituency did not have the political clout to obtain full and immediate funding for PL 94-142.

The upshot of all this was the failure to secure full funding according to the original authorization of expenditures by way of PL 94-142. As it was, by 1979, only about half of the identified handicapped children were being served. Full funding would be necessary to serve them all. It was not forthcoming. Moreover, the BEH claimed that there were many more handicapped children in the States who had not as yet been identified or counted. If they were to be added into the indentified or counted, even more federal funds would be needed. The appropriations record, therefore, was not a good one. Congress not only plays a secondary role to the President in the formulation of the final annual budget, but it has also placed itself under the restraints of having to come in with a final budget that is within the total budget as agreed upon previously through a highly complicated congressional budget process.

The direction that the federal budget takes is in the hands of the President. The Congress originates legislation, but not the federal budget. Congress only reacts to the President's budget, tunes it and adjusts it, but rarely goes beyond it. True enough, the Congress now has its own Congressional Budget Office, but that too is only a reaction to Presidential leadership and serves as a resource aid to the Congress and the Senate and House Budget Committees.

Two major reasons then — funding programs for the handicapped did not have a high priority in the President's Budget and Education was only one part of a much larger Department through 1979 — account for the fact that state and local education agencies did not receive the federal financial assistance they and the handicapped interest groups thought they were due under PL 94-142. Despite the promises made in 1975, when the law was enacted, federal financial assistance to state and local education agencies for the education of all handicapped children did not reach the levels spelled out in the law.

PL 94-142 is a permanent authorization for expenditures and does not have to be renewed every year, but it must be remembered that appropriation of funds is legislated by Congress every year for each succeeding fiscal year. To offset the excess costs of educating handicapped children, PL 94-142 permitted Congress to provide a portion of those costs based on the following formula: up to 5 per cent of the national average per pupil expenditure in public elementary and secondary schools in the United States in fiscal year 1978, increasing 10 per cent every year to a final percentage of 40 per cent in fiscal year 1982 and beyond. (The fiscal year begins on October 1 in the preceding calendar year. Thus FY 1978 began on October 1, 1977, FY 1979 began on October 1, 1978, FY 1980 began on October 1, 1979 etc.) In order for state and local education agencies to plan for their school years, all education programs, including those for handicapped children, are "forward funded." This means that money appropriated by Congress for a specific fiscal year, let us say FY 1981 which begins on October 1, 1980, is to be used by school districts in the school year 1981–82, which begins on September 1, 1981. Schools therefore know how much federal money will be made available to them almost a full year before they are to use it. There is also no one-month lag (September) in receipt of federal funds, because the funds the schools receive for the beginning of the school year have been on tap since the *previous* October. Thus schools can plan ahead in developing programs, hiring staff, purchasing equipment and so forth. Although there is some confusion because of the overlap of fiscal and school years, "forward funding" makes financial sense and also permits the school districts to have some "carry-over" funds left over from the previous school year.

We can now briefly look at the gap between authorized and appropriated funds that developed by 1981. Congressional appropriations for fiscal year 1977 followed the 5 per cent formula of PL 94–142, to start off the program. The sum appropriated was $315 million. FY 1978 appropriations were based on the 10 per cent authorization, one step up as spelled out in PL 94–142. The total amount available was $535 million of which $70 million was a "carry-over" from the previous year. For FY 1979, the Congress had the right, under the provisions of PL 94–142, to use the 20 per cent level. President Carter, however, in his attempt to hold down overall federal spending, requested $804 million for the program, which covered only 12.5 per cent of the excess costs of educating handicapped children being served instead of the 20 per cent authorized by law. Congress accepted this figure and appropriated what the President had requested. The following year, for FY 1980, President Carter proposed that appropriations be $862 million. Congress raised the figure, however, to $874.5 million, amounting to a 12 per cent level whereas PL 94–142 had authorized the increase to 30 per cent. The President had asked for an appropriation which would have kept the percentage pretty much the same as in the previous year. The Congress indeed had added $12.5 million to his budget request, but the intent of PL 94-142 had been to permit the per cent to rise to 30. For both FY 1979 and 1980, Congress had underfunded the education of handicapped children.

The Office of Management and Budget, the creator of the President's Budget, was becoming a difficult barrier for advocates for handicapped children to cross. For FY 1981, when the PL 94-142 authorization reached 40 per cent, the administration requested $922 million for PL 94-142's share of the education budget, which represented a percentage of below 12 per cent. The second session of the 96th Congress in 1980 pretty much held to the President's request. Thus, the percentage remained about 28 points below the authorized 40 per cent.

Although PL 94-142 is still a landmark Act of Congress which continues to have a positive impact on education for handicapped children, its force has been severely lessened because of Congressional underfunding. It does not appear that any President, at least in the near future, will be in a position to recommend to the Congress that PL 94-142 reach full funding. Shifting priorities in the President's budget will work against any significant increase in federal financial assistance for the education of handicapped children. Nor will the Congress be able or willing to force on a President a federal budget that will meet the full 40 per cent level authorized by PL 94-142.

There is one glimmer of hope that full funding might be approached. In 1980, a new Department of Education came into being. The education community might have greater access to OMB and the President than when "Education" was part of the old Health, Education and Welfare Department. If the new Secretary of Education is able to exercise real political "clout," the financial situation for the education of handicapped children might change for the better. A clue depicting the direction the new Department might take will be found in the appropriation requests it makes on behalf of handicapped children of the OMB and the Congress in the first session of the 97th Congress in 1981, and in its relative success in obtaining what it wants from both.

Appendix

Public Law 94-142
94th Congress, S. 6
November 29, 1975

An Act

To amend the Education of the Handicapped Act to provide educational assistance to all handicapped children, and for other purposes.

Be it enacted by the Senate and House of Representatives of the United States of America in Congress assembled, That this Act may be cited as the "Education for All Handicapped Children Act of 1975".

Education for All Handicapped Children Act of 1975. 20 USC 1401 note.

EXTENSION OF EXISTING LAW

SEC. 2. (a)(1)(A) Section 611(b)(2) of the Education of the Handicapped Act (20 U.S.C. 1411(b)(2)) (hereinafter in this Act referred to as the "Act"), as in effect during the fiscal years 1976 and 1977, is amended by striking out "the Commonwealth of Puerto Rico,".

(B) Section 611(c)(1) of the Act (20 U.S.C. 1411(c)(1)), as in effect during the fiscal years 1976 and 1977, is amended by striking out "the Commonwealth of Puerto Rico,".

(2) Section 611(c)(2) of the Act (20 U.S.C. 1411(c)(2)), as in effect during the fiscal years 1976 and 1977, is amended by striking out "year ending June 30, 1975" and inserting in lieu thereof the following: "years ending June 30, 1975, and 1976, and for the fiscal year ending September 30, 1977", and by striking out "2 per centum" each place it appears therein and inserting in lieu thereof "1 per centum".

(3) Section 611(d) of the Act (20 U.S.C. 1411(d)), as in effect during the fiscal years 1976 and 1977, is amended by striking out "year ending June 30, 1975" and inserting in lieu thereof the following: "years ending June 30, 1975, and 1976, and for the fiscal year ending September 30, 1977".

(4) Section 612(a) of the Act (20 U.S.C. 1412(a)), as in effect during the fiscal years 1976 and 1977, is amended—

(A) by striking out "year ending June 30, 1975" and inserting in lieu thereof "years ending June 30, 1975, and 1976, for the period beginning July 1, 1976, and ending September 30, 1976, and for the fiscal year ending September 30, 1977"; and

(B) by striking out "fiscal year 1974" and inserting in lieu thereof "preceding fiscal year".

(b)(1) Section 614(a) of the Education Amendments of 1974 (Public Law 93–380; 88 Stat. 580) is amended by striking out "fiscal year 1975" and inserting in lieu thereof the following: "the fiscal years ending June 30, 1975, and 1976, for the period beginning July 1, 1976, and ending September 30, 1976, and for the fiscal year ending September 30, 1977,".

20 USC 1411 note.

(2) Section 614(b) of the Education Amendments of 1974 (Public Law 93–380; 88 Stat. 580) is amended by striking out "fiscal year 1974" and inserting in lieu thereof the following: "the fiscal years ending June 30. 1975, and 1976, for the period beginning July 1, 1976, and ending September 30, 1976, and for the fiscal year ending September 30, 1977,".

20 USC 1411 note.

Pub. Law 94-142   - 2 -   November 29, 1975

20 USC 1413
note.
(3) Section 614(c) of the Education Amendments of 1974 (Public Law 93-380; 88 Stat. 580) is amended by striking out "fiscal year 1974" and inserting in lieu thereof the following: "the fiscal years ending June 30, 1975, and 1976, for the period beginning July 1, 1976, and ending September 30, 1976, and for the fiscal year ending September 30, 1977,".

Ante, p. 773.
(c) Section 612(a) of the Act, as in effect during the fiscal years 1976 and 1977, and as amended by subsection (a)(4), is amended by inserting immediately before the period at the end thereof the following: ", or $300,000, whichever is greater".

20 USC 1412.
(d) Section 612 of the Act (20 U.S.C. 1411), as in effect during the fiscal years 1976 and 1977, is amended by adding at the end thereof the following new subsection:

Publication in Federal Register.
"(d) The Commissioner shall, no later than one hundred twenty days after the date of the enactment of the Education for All Handicapped Children Act of 1975, prescribe and publish in the Federal Register such rules as he considers necessary to carry out the provisions of this section and section 611.".

Ante, p. 773.
20 USC 1411
note.
(e) Notwithstanding the provisions of section 611 of the Act, as in effect during the fiscal years 1976 and 1977, there are authorized to be appropriated $100,000,000 for the fiscal year 1976, such sums as may be necessary for the period beginning July 1, 1976, and ending September 30, 1976, and $200,000,000 for the fiscal year 1977, to carry out the provisions of part B of the Act, as in effect during such fiscal years.

STATEMENT OF FINDINGS AND PURPOSE

20 USC 1401
note.
SEC. 3. (a) Section 601 of the Act (20 U.S.C. 1401) is amended by inserting "(a)" immediately before "This title" and by adding at the end thereof the following new subsections:

"(b) The Congress finds that—

"(1) there are more than eight million handicapped children in the United States today;

"(2) the special educational needs of such children are not being fully met;

"(3) more than half of the handicapped children in the United States do not receive appropriate educational services which would enable them to have full equality of opportunity;

"(4) one million of the handicapped children in the United States are excluded entirely from the public school system and will not go through the educational process with their peers;

"(5) there are many handicapped children throughout the United States participating in regular school programs whose handicaps prevent them from having a successful educational experience because their handicaps are undetected;

"(6) because of the lack of adequate services within the public school system, families are often forced to find services outside the public school system, often at great distance from their residence and at their own expense;

"(7) developments in the training of teachers and in diagnostic and instructional procedures and methods have advanced to the point that, given appropriate funding, State and local educational agencies can and will provide effective special education and related services to meet the needs of handicapped children;

"(8) State and local educational agencies have a responsibility to provide education for all handicapped children, but present financial resources are inadequate to meet the special educational needs of handicapped children; and

"(9) it is in the national interest that the Federal Government assist State and local efforts to provide programs to meet the educational needs of handicapped children in order to assure equal protection of the law.

"(c) It is the purpose of this Act to assure that all handicapped children have available to them, within the time periods specified in section 612(2)(B), a free appropriate public education which emphasizes special education and related services designed to meet their unique needs, to assure that the rights of handicapped children and their parents or guardians are protected, to assist States and localities to provide for the education of all handicapped children, and to assess and assure the effectiveness of efforts to educate handicapped children.".

(b) The heading for section 601 of the Act (20 U.S.C. 1401) is amended to read as follows:

Ante, p. 773.

"SHORT TITLE; STATEMENT OF FINDINGS AND PURPOSE".

DEFINITIONS

SEC. 4. (a) Section 602 of the Act (20 U.S.C. 1402) is amended—

20 USC 1401.

(1) in paragraph (1) thereof, by striking out "crippled" and inserting in lieu thereof "orthopedically impaired", and by inserting immediately after "impaired children" the following: ", or children with specific learning disabilities,";

(2) in paragraph (5) thereof, by inserting immediately after "instructional materials," the following: "telecommunications, sensory, and other technological aids and devices,";

(3) in the last sentence of paragraph (15) thereof, by inserting immediately after "environmental" the following: ", cultural, or economic"; and

(4) by adding at the end thereof the following new paragraphs:

"(16) The term 'special education' means specially designed instruction, at no cost to parents or guardians, to meet the unique needs of a handicapped child, including classroom instruction, instruction in physical education, home instruction, and instruction in hospitals and institutions.

"(17) The term 'related services' means transportation, and such developmental, corrective, and other supportive services (including speech pathology and audiology, psychological services, physical and occupational therapy, recreation, and medical and counseling services, except that such medical services shall be for diagnostic and evaluation purposes only) as may be required to assist a handicapped child to benefit from special education, and includes the early identification and assessment of handicapping conditions in children.

"(18) The term 'free appropriate public education' means special education and related services which (A) have been provided at public expense, under public supervision and direction, and without charge, (B) meet the standards of the State educational agency, (C) include an appropriate preschool, elementary, or secondary school education in the State involved, and (D) are provided in conformity with the individualized education program required under section 614(a)(5).

Pub. Law 94-142   - 4 -   November 29, 1975

"(19) The term 'individualized education program' means a written statement for each handicapped child developed in any meeting by a representative of the local educational agency or an intermediate educational unit who shall be qualified to provide, or supervise the provision of, specially designed instruction to meet the unique needs of handicapped children, the teacher, the parents or guardian of such child, and, whenever appropriate, such child, which statement shall include (A) a statement of the present levels of educational performance of such child, (B) a statement of annual goals, including short-term instructional objectives, (C) a statement of the specific educational services to be provided to such child, and the extent to which such child will be able to participate in regular educational programs, (D) the projected date for initiation and anticipated duration of such services, and (E) appropriate objective criteria and evaluation procedures and schedules for determining, on at least an annual basis, whether instructional objectives are being achieved.

"(20) The term 'excess costs' means those costs which are in excess of the average annual per student expenditure in a local educational agency during the preceding school year for an elementary or secondary school student, as may be appropriate, and which shall be computed after deducting (A) amounts received under this part or under title I or title VII of the Elementary and Secondary Education Act of 1965, and (B) any State or local funds expended for programs which would qualify for assistance under this part or under such titles.

20 USC 241a note, 881.

"(21) The term 'native language' has the meaning given that term by section 703(a)(2) of the Bilingual Education Act (20 U.S.C. 880b-1(a)(2)).

"(22) The term 'intermediate educational unit' means any public authority, other than a local educational agency, which is under the general supervision of a State educational agency, which is established by State law for the purpose of providing free public education on a regional basis, and which provides special education and related services to handicapped children within that State.".

(b) The heading for section 602 of the Act (20 U.S.C. 1402) is amended to read as follows:

"DEFINITIONS".

ASSISTANCE FOR EDUCATION OF ALL HANDICAPPED CHILDREN

SEC. 5. (a) Part B of the Act (20 U.S.C. 1411 et seq.) is amended to read as follows:

"PART B—ASSISTANCE FOR EDUCATION OF ALL HANDICAPPED CHILDREN

"ENTITLEMENTS AND ALLOCATIONS

20 USC 1411. Post, p. 793.

"SEC. 611. (a)(1) Except as provided in paragraph (3) and in section 619, the maximum amount of the grant to which a State is entitled under this part for any fiscal year shall be equal to—

"(A) the number of handicapped children aged three to twenty-one, inclusive, in such State who are receiving special education and related services;
multiplied by—

"(B)(i) 5 per centum, for the fiscal year ending September 30, 1978, of the average per pupil expenditure in public elementary and secondary schools in the United States;

194

"(ii) 10 per centum, for the fiscal year ending September 30, 1979, of the average per pupil expenditure in public elementary and secondary schools in the United States;

"(iii) 20 per centum, for the fiscal year ending September 30, 1980, of the average per pupil expenditure in public elementary and secondary schools in the United States;

"(iv) 30 per centum, for the fiscal year ending September 30, 1981, of the average per pupil expenditure in public elementary and secondary schools in the United States; and

"(v) 40 per centum, for the fiscal year ending September 30, 1982, and for each fiscal year thereafter, of the average per pupil expenditure in public elementary and secondary schools in the United States;

except that no State shall receive an amount which is less than the amount which such State received under this part for the fiscal year ending September 30, 1977.

"(2) For the purpose of this subsection and subsection (b) through subsection (e), the term 'State' does not include Guam, American Samoa, the Virgin Islands, and the Trust Territory of the Pacific Islands.

"State. "

"(3) The number of handicapped children receiving special education and related services in any fiscal year shall be equal to the average of the number of such children receiving special education and related services on October 1 and February 1 of the fiscal year preceding the fiscal year for which the determination is made.

"(4) For purposes of paragraph (1)(B), the term 'average per pupil expenditure', in the United States, means the aggregate current expenditures, during the second fiscal year preceding the fiscal year for which the computation is made (or, if satisfactory data for such year are not available at the time of computation, then during the most recent preceding fiscal year for which satisfactory data are available) of all local educational agencies in the United States (which, for purposes of this subsection, means the fifty States and the District of Columbia), as the case may be, plus any direct expenditures by the State for operation of such agencies (without regard to the source of funds from which either of such expenditures are made), divided by the aggregate number of children in average daily attendance to whom such agencies provided free public education during such preceding year.

"Average per pupil expenditure. "

"(5)(A) In determining the allotment of each State under paragraph (1), the Commissioner may not count—

"(i) handicapped children in such State under paragraph (1) (A) to the extent the number of such children is greater than 12 per centum of the number of all children aged five to seventeen, inclusive, in such State;

"(ii) as part of such percentage, children with specific learning disabilities to the extent the number of such children is greater than one-sixth of such percentage; and

"(iii) handicapped children who are counted under section 121 of the Elementary and Secondary Education Act of 1965.

20 USC 241c-1.

"(B) For purposes of subparagraph (A), the number of children aged five to seventeen, inclusive, in any State shall be determined by the Commissioner on the basis of the most recent satisfactory data available to him.

"(b) (1) Of the funds received under subsection (a) by any State for the fiscal year ending September 30, 1978—

"(A) 50 per centum of such funds may be used by such State in accordance with the provisions of paragraph (2) ; and

"(B) 50 per centum of such funds shall be distributed by such State pursuant to subsection (d) to local educational agencies and intermediate educational units in such State, for use in accordance with the priorities established under section 612(3).

"(2) Of the funds which any State may use under paragraph (1) (A)—

"(A) an amount which is equal to the greater of—

"(i) 5 per centum of the total amount of funds received under this part by such State ; or

"(ii) $200,000;

may be used by such State for administrative costs related to carrying out sections 612 and 613 ;

"(B) the remainder shall be used by such State to provide support services and direct services, in accordance with the priorities established under section 612(3).

"(c) (1) Of the funds received under subsection (a) by any State for the fiscal year ending September 30, 1979, and for each fiscal year thereafter—

"(A) 25 per centum of such funds may be used by such State in accordance with the provisions of paragraph (2) ; and

"(B) except as provided in paragraph (3), 75 per centum of such funds shall be distributed by such State pursuant to subsection (d) to local educational agencies and intermediate educational units in such State, for use in accordance with priorities established under section 612(3).

"(2) (A) Subject to the provisions of subparagraph (B), of the funds which any State may use under paragraph (1) (A)—

"(i) an amount which is equal to the greater of—

"(I) 5 per centum of the total amount of funds received under this part by such State ; or

"(II) $200,000;

may be used by such State for administrative costs related to carrying out the provisions of sections 612 and 613 ; and

"(ii) the remainder shall be used by such State to provide support services and direct services, in accordance with the priorities established under section 612(3).

"(B) The amount expended by any State from the funds available to such State under paragraph (1) (A) in any fiscal year for the provision of support services or for the provision of direct services shall be matched on a program basis by such State, from funds other than Federal funds, for the provision of support services or for the provision of direct services for the fiscal year involved.

"(3) The provisions of section 613(a) (9) shall not apply with respect to amounts available for use by any State under paragraph (2).

"(4) (A) No funds shall be distributed by any State under this subsection in any fiscal year to any local educational agency or intermediate educational unit in such State if—

"(i) such local educational agency or intermediate educational unit is entitled, under subsection (d), to less than $7,500 for such fiscal year ; or

"(ii) such local educational agency or intermediate educational unit has not submitted an application for such funds which meets the requirements of section 614.

"(B) Whenever the provisions of subparagraph (A) apply, the State involved shall use such funds to assure the provision of a free appropriate education to handicapped children residing in the area served by such local educational agency or such intermediate educational unit. The provisions of paragraph (2)(B) shall not apply to the use of such funds.

"(d) From the total amount of funds available to local educational agencies and intermediate educational units in any State under subsection (b)(1)(B) or subsection (c)(1)(B), as the case may be, each local educational agency or intermediate educational unit shall be entitled to an amount which bears the same ratio to the total amount available under subsection (b)(1)(B) or subsection (c)(1)(B), as the case may be, as the number of handicapped children aged three to twenty-one, inclusive, receiving special education and related services in such local educational agency or intermediate educational unit bears to the aggregate number of handicapped children aged three to twenty-one, inclusive, receiving special education and related services in all local educational agencies and intermediate educational units which apply to the State educational agency involved for funds under this part.

"(e)(1) The jurisdictions to which this subsection applies are Guam, American Samoa, the Virgin Islands, and the Trust Territory of the Pacific Islands.

"(2) Each jurisdiction to which this subsection applies shall be entitled to a grant for the purposes set forth in section 601(c) in an amount equal to an amount determined by the Commissioner in accordance with criteria based on respective needs, except that the aggregate of the amount to which such jurisdictions are so entitled for any fiscal year shall not exceed an amount equal to 1 per centum of the aggregate of the amounts available to all States under this part for that fiscal year. If the aggregate of the amounts, determined by the Commissioner pursuant to the preceding sentence, to be so needed for any fiscal year exceeds an amount equal to such 1 per centum limitation, the entitlement of each such jurisdiction shall be reduced proportionately until such aggregate does not exceed such 1 per centum limitation.   *Ante*, **p. 774.**

"(3) The amount expended for administration by each jurisdiction under this subsection shall not exceed 5 per centum of the amount allotted to such jurisdiction for any fiscal year, or $35,000, whichever is greater.

"(f)(1) The Commissioner is authorized to make payments to the Secretary of the Interior according to the need for such assistance for the education of handicapped children on reservations serviced by elementary and secondary schools operated for Indian children by the Department of the Interior. The amount of such payment for any fiscal year shall not exceed 1 per centum of the aggregate amounts available to all States under this part for that fiscal year.

"(2) The Secretary of the Interior may receive an allotment under this subsection only after submitting to the Commissioner an application which meets the applicable requirements of section 614(a) and which is approved by the Commissioner. The provisions of section 616 shall apply to any such application.

"(g)(1) If the sums appropriated for any fiscal year for making payments to States under this part are not sufficient to pay in full the total amounts which all States are entitled to receive under this part for such fiscal year, the maximum amounts which all States are entitled to receive under this part for such fiscal year shall be ratably reduced. In case additional funds become available for making such payments for any fiscal year during which the preceding sentence is applicable, such reduced amounts shall be increased on the same basis as they were reduced.

"(2) In the case of any fiscal year in which the maximum amounts for which States are eligible have been reduced under the first sentence of paragraph (1), and in which additional funds have not been made available to pay in full the total of such maximum amounts under the last sentence of such paragraph, the State educational agency shall fix dates before which each local educational agency or intermediate educational unit shall report to the State educational agency on the amount of funds available to the local educational agency or intermediate educational unit, under the provisions of subsection (d), which it estimates that it will expend in accordance with the provisions of this part. The amounts so available to any local educational agency or intermediate educational unit, or any amount which would be available to any other local educational agency or intermediate educational unit if it were to submit a program meeting the requirements of this part, which the State educational agency determines will not be used for the period of its availability, shall be available for allocation to those local educational agencies or intermediate educational units, in the manner provided by this section, which the State educational agency determines will need and be able to use additional funds to carry out approved programs.

"ELIGIBILITY

20 USC 1412.

"SEC. 612. In order to qualify for assistance under this part in any fiscal year, a State shall demonstrate to the Commissioner that the following conditions are met:

"(1) The State has in effect a policy that assures all handicapped children the right to a free appropriate public education.

"(2) The State has developed a plan pursuant to section 613(b) in effect prior to the date of the enactment of the Education for All Handicapped Children Act of 1975 and submitted not later than August 21, 1975, which will be amended so as to comply with the provisions of this paragraph. Each such amended plan shall set forth in detail the policies and procedures which the State will undertake or has undertaken in order to assure that—

"(A) there is established (i) a goal of providing full educational opportunity to all handicapped children, (ii) a detailed timetable for accomplishing such a goal, and (iii) a description of the kind and number of facilities, personnel, and services necessary throughout the State to meet such a goal;

"(B) a free appropriate public education will be available for all handicapped children between the ages of three and eighteen within the State not later than September 1, 1978, and for all handicapped children between the ages of three and twenty-one within the State not later than September 1, 1980, except that, with respect to handicapped children aged three to five and aged eighteen to twenty-one, inclusive, the requirements of this clause shall not be applied in any State if the application of such requirements would be inconsistent with State law or practice, or the order of any court, respecting public education within such age groups in the State;

"(C) all children residing in the State who are handicapped, regardless of the severity of their handicap. and who are in need of special education and related services are identified, located, and evaluated, and that a practical method is developed and implemented to determine which children are currently receiving needed special education and related services and which children are not currently receiving needed special education and related services;

"(D) policies and procedures are established in accordance with detailed criteria prescribed under section 617(c) ; and

"(E) the amendment to the plan submitted by the State required by this section shall be available to parents, guardians, and other members of the general public at least thirty days prior to the date of submission of the amendment to the Commissioner.

"(3) The State has established priorities for providing a free appropriate public education to all handicapped children, which priorities shall meet the timetables set forth in clause (B) of paragraph (2) of this section, first with respect to handicapped children who are not receiving an education, and second with respect to handicapped children, within each disability, with the most severe handicaps who are receiving an inadequate education. and has made adequate progress in meeting the timetables set forth in clause (B) of paragraph (2) of this section.

"(4) Each local educational agency in the State will maintain records of the individualized education program for each handicapped child, and such program shall be established, reviewed, and revised as provided in section 614(a)(5).

"(5) The State has established (A) procedural safeguards as required by section 615, (B) procedures to assure that, to the maximum extent appropriate, handicapped children, including children in public or private institutions or other care facilities, are educated with children who are not handicapped, and that special classes, separate schooling, or other removal of handicapped children from the regular educational environment occurs only when the nature or severity of the handicap is such that education in regular classes with the use of supplementary aids and services cannot be achieved satisfactorily, and (C) procedures to assure that testing and evaluation materials and procedures utilized for the purposes of evaluation and placement of handicapped children will be selected and administered so as not to be racially or culturally discriminatory. Such materials or procedures shall be provided and administered in the child's native language or mode of communication, unless it clearly is not feasible to do so, and no single procedure shall be the sole criterion for determining an appropriate educational program for a child.

"(6) The State educational agency shall be responsible for assuring   Administration. that the requirements of this part are carried out and that all educational programs for handicapped children within the State, including all such programs administered by any other State or local agency, will be under the general supervision of the persons responsible for educational programs for handicapped children in the State educational agency and shall meet education standards of the State educational agency.

Notice,
hearings.

"(7) The State shall assure that (A) in carrying out the requirements of this section procedures are established for consultation with individuals involved in or concerned with the education of handicapped children, including handicapped individuals and parents or guardians of handicapped children, and (B) there are public hearings, adequate notice of such hearings, and an opportunity for comment available to the general public prior to adoption of the policies, programs, and procedures required pursuant to the provisions of this section and section 613.

"STATE PLANS

20 USC 1413.

"SEC. 613. (a) Any State meeting the eligibility requirements set forth in section 612 and desiring to participate in the program under this part shall submit to the Commissioner, through its State educational agency, a State plan at such time, in such manner, and containing or accompanied by such information, as he deems necessary. Each such plan shall—

"(1) set forth policies and procedures designed to assure that funds paid to the State under this part will be expended in accordance with the provisions of this part, with particular attention given to the provisions of sections 611(b), 611(c), 611(d), 612(2), and 612(3);

"(2) provide that programs and procedures will be established to assure that funds received by the State or any of its political subdivisions under any other Federal program, including section 121 of the Elementary and Secondary Education Act of 1965 (20

20 USC 241c-1.

U.S.C. 241c-2), section 305(b)(8) of such Act (20 U.S.C. 844a (b)(8)) or its successor authority, and section 122(a)(4)(B) of the Vocational Education Act of 1963 (20 U.S.C. 1262(a)(4) (B)), under which there is specific authority for the provision of assistance for the education of handicapped children, will be utilized by the State, or any of its political subdivisions, only in a manner consistent with the goal of providing a free appropriate public education for all handicapped children, except that nothing in this clause shall be construed to limit the specific requirements of the laws governing such Federal programs;

"(3) set forth, consistent with the purposes of this Act, a description of programs and procedures for (A) the development and implementation of a comprehensive system of personnel development which shall include the inservice training of general and special educational instructional and support personnel, detailed procedures to assure that all personnel necessary to carry out the purposes of this Act are appropriately and adequately prepared and trained, and effective procedures for acquiring and disseminating to teachers and administrators of programs for handicapped children significant information derived from educational research, demonstration, and similar projects, and (B) adopting, where appropriate, promising educational practices and materials development through such projects;

"(4) set forth policies and procedures to assure—

"(A) that, to the extent consistent with the number and location of handicapped children in the State who are enrolled in private elementary and secondary schools, provision is made for the participation of such children in the program assisted or carried out under this part by providing for such children special education and related services; and

"(B) that (i) handicapped children in private schools and facilities will be provided special education and related services (in conformance with an individualized educational program as required by this part) at no cost to their parents or guardian, if such children are placed in or referred to such schools or facilities by the State or appropriate local educational agency as the means of carrying out the requirements of this part or any other applicable law requiring the provision of special education and related services to all handicapped children within such State, and (ii) in all such instances the State educational agency shall determine whether such schools and facilities meet standards that apply to State and local educational agencies and that children so served have all the rights they would have if served by such agencies;

"(5) set forth policies and procedures which assure that the State shall seek to recover any funds made available under this part for services to any child who is determined to be erroneously classified as eligible to be counted under section 611(a) or section 611(d);

"(6) provide satisfactory assurance that the control of funds provided under this part, and title to property derived therefrom, shall be in a public agency for the uses and purposes provided in this part, and that a public agency will administer such funds and property;

"(7) provide for (A) making such reports in such form and containing such information as the Commissioner may require to carry out his functions under this part, and (B) keeping such records and affording such access thereto as the Commissioner may find necessary to assure the correctness and verification of such reports and proper disbursement of Federal funds under this part; **Reports and records.**

"(8) provide procedures to assure that final action with respect to any application submitted by a local educational agency or an intermediate educational unit shall not be taken without first affording the local educational agency or intermediate educational unit involved reasonable notice and opportunity for a hearing; **Notice, hearings.**

"(9) provide satisfactory assurance that Federal funds made available under this part (A) will not be commingled with State funds, and (B) will be so used as to supplement and increase the level of State and local funds expended for the education of handicapped children and in no case to supplant such State and local funds, except that, where the State provides clear and convincing evidence that all handicapped children have available to them a free appropriate public education, the Commissioner may waive in part the requirement of this clause if he concurs with the evidence provided by the State;

"(10) provide, consistent with procedures prescribed pursuant to section 617(a)(2), satisfactory assurance that such fiscal control and fund accounting procedures will be adopted as may be necessary to assure proper disbursement of, and accounting for, Federal funds paid under this part to the State, including any such funds paid by the State to local educational agencies and intermediate educational units;

Pub. Law 94-142   - 12 -   November 29, 1975

Evaluation.

"(11) provide for procedures for evaluation at least annually of the effectiveness of programs in meeting the educational needs of handicapped children (including evaluation of individualized education programs), in accordance with such criteria that the Commissioner shall prescribe pursuant to section 617; and

State advisory panel.

"(12) provide that the State has an advisory panel, appointed by the Governor or any other official authorized under State law to make such appointments, composed of individuals involved in or concerned with the education of handicapped children, including handicapped individuals, teachers, parents or guardians of handicapped children, State and local education officials, and administrators of programs for handicapped children, which (A) advises the State educational agency of unmet needs within the State in the education of handicapped children, (B) comments publicly on any rules or regulations proposed for issuance by the State regarding the education of handicapped children and the procedures for distribution of funds under this part, and (C) assists the State in developing and reporting such data and evaluations as may assist the Commissioner in the performance of his responsibilities under section 618.

"(b) Whenever a State educational agency provides free appropriate public education for handicapped children, or provides direct services to such children, such State educational agency shall include, as part of the State plan required by subsection (a) of this section, such additional assurances not specified in such subsection (a) as are contained in section 614(a), except that funds available for the provision of such education or services may be expended without regard to the provisions relating to excess costs in section 614(a).

"(c) The Commissioner shall approve any State plan and any modification thereof which—

"(1) is submitted by a State eligible in accordance with section 612; and

"(2) meets the requirements of subsection (a) and subsection (b).

Notice, hearings.

The Commissioner shall disapprove any State plan which does not meet the requirements of the preceding sentence, but shall not finally disapprove a State plan except after reasonable notice and opportunity for a hearing to the State.

"APPLICATION

20 USC 1414.

"SEC. 614. (a) A local educational agency or an intermediate educational unit which desires to receive payments under section 611(d) for any fiscal year shall submit an application to the appropriate State educational agency. Such application shall—

"(1) provide satisfactory assurance that payments under this part will be used for excess costs directly attributable to programs which—

"(A) provide that all children residing within the jurisdiction of the local educational agency or the intermediate educational unit who are handicapped, regardless of the severity of their handicap, and are in need of special education and related services will be identified, located, and evaluated, and provide for the inclusion of a practical method of determining which children are currently receiving needed special education and related services and which children are not currently receiving such education and services;

"(B) establish policies and procedures in accordance with detailed criteria prescribed under section 617(c);

"(C) establish a goal of providing full educational opportunities to all handicapped children, including—

"(i) procedures for the implementation and use of the comprehensive system of personnel development established by the State educational agency under section 613(a)(3);

"(ii) the provision of, and the establishment of priorities for providing, a free appropriate public education to all handicapped children, first with respect to handicapped children who are not receiving an education, and second with respect to handicapped children, within each disability, with the most severe handicaps who are receiving an inadequate education;

"(iii) the participation and consultation of the parents or guardian of such children; and

"(iv) to the maximum extent practicable and consistent with the provisions of section 612(5)(B), the provision of special services to enable such children to participate in regular educational programs;

"(D) establish a detailed timetable for accomplishing the goal described in subclause (C); and

"(E) provide a description of the kind and number of facilities, personnel, and services necessary to meet the goal described in subclause (C);

"(2) provide satisfactory assurance that (A) the control of funds provided under this part, and title to property derived from such funds, shall be in a public agency for the uses and purposes provided in this part, and that a public agency will administer such funds and property, (B) Federal funds expended by local educational agencies and intermediate educational units for programs under this part (i) shall be used to pay only the excess costs directly attributable to the education of handicapped children, and (ii) shall be used to supplement and, to the extent practicable, increase the level of State and local funds expended for the education of handicapped children, and in no case to supplant such State and local funds, and (C) State and local funds will be used in the jurisdiction of the local educational agency or intermediate educational unit to provide services in program areas which, taken as a whole, are at least comparable to services being provided in areas of such jurisdiction which are not receiving funds under this part;

"(3)(A) provide for furnishing such information (which, in the case of reports relating to performance, is in accordance with specific performance criteria related to program objectives), as may be necessary to enable the State educational agency to perform its duties under this part, including information relating to the educational achievement of handicapped children participating in programs carried out under this part; and

"(B) provide for keeping such records, and provide for affording such access to such records, as the State educational agency may find necessary to assure the correctness and verification of such information furnished under subclause (A); **Recordkeeping.**

"(4) provide for making the application and all pertinent documents related to such application available to parents, guardians, and other members of the general public, and provide that all evaluations and reports required under clause (3) shall be public information; **Public information, availability.**

Appendix

"(5) provide assurances that the local educational agency or intermediate educational unit will establish, or revise, whichever is appropriate, an individualized education program for each handicapped child at the beginning of each school year and will then review and, if appropriate revise, its provisions periodically, but not less than annually;

"(6) provide satisfactory assurance that policies and programs established and administered by the local educational agency or intermediate educational unit shall be consistent with the provisions of paragraph (1) through paragraph (7) of section 612 and section 613(a); and

"(7) provide satisfactory assurance that the local educational agency or intermediate educational unit will establish and maintain procedural safeguards in accordance with the provisions of sections 612(5)(B), 612(5)(C), and 615.

Application approval. "(b)(1) A State educational agency shall approve any application submitted by a local educational agency or an intermediate educational unit under subsection (a) if the State educational agency determines that such application meets the requirements of subsection (a), except that no such application may be approved until the State plan submitted by such State educational agency under subsection (a) is approved by the Commissioner under section 613(c). A State educational agency shall disapprove any application submitted by a local educational agency or an intermediate educational unit under subsection (a) if the State educational agency determines that such application does not meet the requirements of subsection (a).

Notice, hearing. "(2)(A) Whenever a State educational agency, after reasonable notice and opportunity for a hearing, finds that a local educational agency or an intermediate educational unit, in the administration of an application approved by the State educational agency under paragraph (1), has failed to comply with any requirement set forth in such application, the State educational agency, after giving appropriate notice to the local educational agency or the intermediate educational unit, shall—

"(i) make no further payments to such local educational agency or such intermediate educational unit under section 620 until the State educational agency is satisfied that there is no longer any failure to comply with the requirement involved; or

"(ii) take such finding into account in its review of any application made by such local educational agency or such intermediate educational unit under subsection (a).

"(B) The provisions of the last sentence of section 616(a) shall apply to any local educational agency or any intermediate educational unit receiving any notification from a State educational agency under this paragraph.

"(3) In carrying out its functions under paragraph (1), each State educational agency shall consider any decision made pursuant to a hearing held under section 615 which is adverse to the local educational agency or intermediate educational unit involved in such decision.

"(c)(1) A State educational agency may, for purposes of the consideration and approval of applications under this section, require local educational agencies to submit a consolidated application for payments if such State educational agency determines that any individual application submitted by any such local educational agency will be disapproved because such local educational agency is ineligible

to receive payments because of the application of section 611(c)(4)
(A)(i) or such local educational agency would be unable to establish
and maintain programs of sufficient size and scope to effectively meet
the educational needs of handicapped children.

"(2)(A) In any case in which a consolidated application of local
educational agencies is approved by a State educational agency under
paragraph (1), the payments which such local educational agencies
may receive shall be equal to the sum of payments to which each such
local educational agency would be entitled under section 611(d) if an
individual application of any such local educational agency had been
approved.

"(B) The State educational agency shall prescribe rules and regula- **Rules and**
tions with respect to consolidated applications submitted under this **regulations.**
subsection which are consistent with the provisions of paragraph (1)
through paragraph (7) of section 612 and section 613(a) and which
provide participating local educational agencies with joint responsibilities for implementing programs receiving payments under this
part.

"(C) In any case in which an intermediate educational unit is
required pursuant to State law to carry out the provisions of this part,
the joint responsibilities given to local educational agencies under subparagraph (B) shall not apply to the administration and disbursement of any payments received by such intermediate educational unit.
Such responsibilities shall be carried out exclusively by such intermediate educational unit.

"(d) Whenever a State educational agency determines that a local
educational agency—

   "(1) is unable or unwilling to establish and maintain programs
   of free appropriate public education which meet the requirements
   established in subsection (a);

   "(2) is unable or unwilling to be consolidated with other local
   educational agencies in order to establish and maintain such programs; or

   "(3) has one or more handicapped children who can best be
   served by a regional or State center designed to meet the needs of
   such children;

the State educational agency shall use the payments which would
have been available to such local educational agency to provide special
education and related services directly to handicapped children residing in the area served by such local educational agency. The State
educational agency may provide such education and services in such
manner, and at such locations (including regional or State centers),
as it considers appropriate, except that the manner in which such
education and services are provided shall be consistent with the requirements of this part.

"(e) Whenever a State educational agency determines that a local **Funds,**
educational agency is adequately providing a free appropriate public **reallocation.**
education to all handicapped children residing in the area served by
such agency with State and local funds otherwise available to such
agency, the State educational agency may reallocate funds (or such
portion of those funds as may not be required to provide such education and services) made available to such agency, pursuant to section
611(d), to such other local educational agencies within the State as
are not adequately providing special education and related services
to all handicapped children residing in the areas served by such other
local educational agencies.

"(f) Notwithstanding the provisions of subsection (a)(2)(B)(ii), any local educational agency which is required to carry out any program for the education of handicapped children pursuant to a State law shall be entitled to receive payments under section 611(d) for use in carrying out such program, except that such payments may not be used to reduce the level of expenditures for such program made by such local educational agency from State or local funds below the level of such expenditures for the fiscal year prior to the fiscal year for which such local educational agency seeks such payments.

"PROCEDURAL SAFEGUARDS

20 USC 1415.

"SEC. 615. (a) Any State educational agency, any local educational agency, and any intermediate educational unit which receives assistance under this part shall establish and maintain procedures in accordance with subsection (b) through subsection (e) of this section to assure that handicapped children and their parents or guardians are guaranteed procedural safeguards with respect to the provision of free appropriate public education by such agencies and units.

"(b)(1) The procedures required by this section shall include, but shall not be limited to—

"(A) an opportunity for the parents or guardian of a handicapped child to examine all relevant records with respect to the identification, evaluation, and educational placement of the child, and the provision of a free appropriate public education to such child, and to obtain an independent educational evaluation of the child;

"(B) procedures to protect the rights of the child whenever the parents or guardian of the child are not known, unavailable, or the child is a ward of the State, including the assignment of an individual (who shall not be an employee of the State educational agency, local educational agency, or intermediate educational unit involved in the education or care of the child) to act as a surrogate for the parents or guardian;

"(C) written prior notice to the parents or guardian of the child whenever such agency or unit—

"(i) proposes to initiate or change, or

"(ii) refuses to initiate or change,

the identification, evaluation, or educational placement of the child or the provision of a free appropriate public education to the child;

"(D) procedures designed to assure that the notice required by clause (C) fully inform the parents or guardian, in the parents' or guardian's native language, unless it clearly is not feasible to do so, of all procedures available pursuant to this section; and

"(E) an opportunity to present complaints with respect to any matter relating to the identification, evaluation, or educational placement of the child, or the provision of a free appropriate public education to such child.

Hearing.

"(2) Whenever a complaint has been received under paragraph (1) of this subsection, the parents or guardian shall have an opportunity for an impartial due process hearing which shall be conducted by the State educational agency or by the local educational agency or intermediate educational unit, as determined by State law or by the State educational agency. No hearing conducted pursuant to the requirements of this paragraph shall be conducted by an employee of such agency or unit involved in the education or care of the child.

"(c) If the hearing required in paragraph (2) of subsection (b) of this section is conducted by a local educational agency or an intermediate educational unit, any party aggrieved by the findings and decision rendered in such a hearing may appeal to the State educational agency which shall conduct an impartial review of such hearing. The officer conducting such review shall make an independent decision upon completion of such review.

"(d) Any party to any hearing conducted pursuant to subsections (b) and (c) shall be accorded (1) the right to be accompanied and advised by counsel and by individuals with special knowledge or training with respect to the problems of handicapped children, (2) the right to present evidence and confront, cross-examine, and compel the attendance of witnesses, (3) the right to a written or electronic verbatim record of such hearing, and (4) the right to written findings of fact and decisions (which findings and decisions shall also be transmitted to the advisory panel established pursuant to section 613(a)(12)).

"(e)(1) A decision made in a hearing conducted pursuant to paragraph (2) of subsection (b) shall be final, except that any party involved in such hearing may appeal such decision under the provisions of subsection (c) and paragraph (2) of this subsection. A decision made under subsection (c) shall be final, except that any party may bring an action under paragraph (2) of this subsection.

"(2) Any party aggrieved by the findings and decision made under subsection (b) who does not have the right to an appeal under subsection (c), and any party aggrieved by the findings and decision under subsection (c), shall have the right to bring a civil action with respect to the complaint presented pursuant to this section, which action may be brought in any State court of competent jurisdiction or in a district court of the United States without regard to the amount in controversy. In any action brought under this paragraph the court shall receive the records of the administrative proceedings, shall hear additional evidence at the request of a party, and, basing its decision on the preponderance of the evidence, shall grant such relief as the court determines is appropriate. *Civil action.*

"(3) During the pendency of any proceedings conducted pursuant to this section, unless the State or local educational agency and the parents or guardian otherwise agree, the child shall remain in the then current educational placement of such child, or, if applying for initial admission to a public school, shall, with the consent of the parents or guardian, be placed in the public school program until all such proceedings have been completed.

"(4) The district courts of the United States shall have jurisdiction of actions brought under this subsection without regard to the amount in controversy. *District courts jurisdiction.*

"WITHHOLDING AND JUDICIAL REVIEW

"SEC. 616. (a) Whenever the Commissioner, after reasonable notice and opportunity for hearing to the State educational agency involved (and to any local educational agency or intermediate educational unit affected by any failure described in clause (2)), finds— *Notice, hearing. 20 USC 1416.*

"(1) that there has been a failure to comply substantially with any provision of section 612 or section 613, or

Pub. Law 94-142   - 18 -   November 29, 1975

"(2) that in the administration of the State plan there is a failure to comply with any provision of this part or with any requirements set forth in the application of a local educational agency or intermediate educational unit approved by the State educational agency pursuant to the State plan,
the Commissioner (A) shall, after notifying the State educational agency, withhold any further payments to the State under this part, and (B) may, after notifying the State educational agency, withhold further payments to the State under the Federal programs specified in section 613(a)(2) within his jurisdiction, to the extent that funds under such programs are available for the provision of assistance for the education of handicapped children. If the Commissioner withholds further payments under clause (A) or clause (B) he may determine that such withholding will be limited to programs or projects under the State plan, or portions thereof, affected by the failure, or that the State educational agency shall not make further payments under this part to specified local educational agencies or intermediate educational units affected by the failure. Until the Commissioner is satisfied that there is no longer any failure to comply with the provisions of this part, as specified in clause (1) or clause (2), no further payments shall be made to the State under this part or under the Federal programs specified in section 613(a)(2) within his jurisdiction to the extent that funds under such programs are available for the provision of assistance for the education of handicapped children, or payments by the State educational agency under this part shall be limited to local educational agencies and intermediate educational units whose actions did not cause or were not involved in the failure, as the case may be. Any State educational agency, local educational agency, or intermediate educational unit in receipt of a notice pursuant to the first sentence of this subsection shall, by means of a public notice, take such measures as may be necessary to bring the pendency of an action pursuant to this subsection to the attention of the public within the jurisdiction of such agency or unit.

Petition for review. "(b)(1) If any State is dissatisfied with the Commissioner's final action with respect to its State plan submitted under section 613, such State may, within sixty days after notice of such action, file with the United States court of appeals for the circuit in which such State is located a petition for review of that action. A copy of the petition shall be forthwith transmitted by the clerk of the court to the Commissioner. The Commissioner thereupon shall file in the court the record of the proceedings on which he based his action, as provided in section 2112 of title 28, United States Code.

"(2) The findings of fact by the Commissioner, if supported by substantial evidence, shall be conclusive; but the court, for good cause shown, may remand the case to the Commissioner to take further evidence, and the Commissioner may thereupon make new or modified findings of fact and may modify his previous action, and shall file in the court the record of the further proceedings. Such new or modified findings of fact shall likewise be conclusive if supported by substantial evidence.

"(3) Upon the filing of such petition, the court shall have jurisdiction to affirm the action of the Commissioner or to set it aside, in whole or in part. The judgment of the court shall be subject to review by the Supreme Court of the United States upon certiorari or certification as provided in section 1254 of title 28, United States Code.

"ADMINISTRATION

"SEC. 617. (a)(1) In carrying out his duties under this part, the Commissioner shall—   20 USC 1417.
   "(A) cooperate with, and furnish all technical assistance necessary, directly or by grant or contract, to the States in matters relating to the education of handicapped children and the execution of the provisions of this part;
   "(B) provide such short-term training programs and institutes as are necessary;
   "(C) disseminate information, and otherwise promote the education of all handicapped children within the States; and
   "(D) assure that each State shall, within one year after the date of the enactment of the Education for All Handicapped Children Act of 1975, provide certification of the actual number of handicapped children receiving special education and related services in such State.

"(2) As soon as practicable after the date of the enactment of the Education for All Handicapped Children Act of 1975, the Commissioner shall, by regulation, prescribe a uniform financial report to be utilized by State educational agencies in submitting State plans under this part in order to assure equity among the States.   Regulations.

"(b) In carrying out the provisions of this part, the Commissioner (and the Secretary, in carrying out the provisions of subsection (c)) shall issue, not later than January 1, 1977, amend, and revoke such rules and regulations as may be necessary. No other less formal method of implementing such provisions is authorized.

"(c) The Secretary shall take appropriate action, in accordance with the provisions of section 438 of the General Education Provisions Act, to assure the protection of the confidentiality of any personally identifiable data, information, and records collected or maintained by the Commissioner and by State and local educational agencies pursuant to the provisions of this part.   20 USC 1232g.

"(d) The Commissioner is authorized to hire qualified personnel necessary to conduct data collection and evaluation activities required by subsections (b), (c) and (d) of section 618 and to carry out his duties under subsection (a)(1) of this subsection without regard to the provisions of title 5, United States Code, relating to appointments in the competitive service and without regard to chapter 51 and subchapter III of chapter 53 of such title relating to classification and general schedule pay rates except that no more than twenty such personnel shall be employed at any time.   5 USC 5101, 5331.

"EVALUATION

"SEC. 618. (a) The Commissioner shall measure and evaluate the impact of the program authorized under this part and the effectiveness of State efforts to assure the free appropriate public education of all handicapped children.   20 USC 1418.

"(b) The Commissioner shall conduct, directly or by grant or contract, such studies, investigations, and evaluations as are necessary to assure effective implementation of this part. In carrying out his responsibilities under this section, the Commissioner shall—
   "(1) through the National Center for Education Statistics, provide to the appropriate committees of each House of the Congress and to the general public at least annually, and shall update at least annually, programmatic information concerning programs and projects assisted under this part and other Federal programs

supporting the education of handicapped children, and such information from State and local educational agencies and other appropriate sources necessary for the implementation of this part, including—

"(A) the number of handicapped children in each State, within each disability, who require special education and related services;

"(B) the number of handicapped children in each State, within each disability, receiving a free appropriate public education and the number of handicapped children who need and are not receiving a free appropriate public education in each such State;

"(C) the number of handicapped children in each State, within each disability, who are participating in regular educational programs, consistent with the requirements of section 612(5)(B) and section 614(a)(1)(C)(iv), and the number of handicapped children who have been placed in separate classes or separate school facilities, or who have been otherwise removed from the regular education environment;

"(D) the number of handicapped children who are enrolled in public or private institutions in each State and who are receiving a free appropriate public education, and the number of handicapped children who are in such institutions and who are not receiving a free appropriate public education;

"(E) the amount of Federal, State, and local expenditures in each State specifically available for special education and related services; and

"(F) the number of personnel, by disability category, employed in the education of handicapped children, and the estimated number of additional personnel needed to adequately carry out the policy established by this Act; and

"(2) provide for the evaluation of programs and projects assisted under this part through—

"(A) the development of effective methods and procedures for evaluation;

"(B) the testing and validation of such evaluation methods and procedures; and

"(C) conducting actual evaluation studies designed to test the effectiveness of such programs and projects.

"(c) In developing and furnishing information under subclause (E) of clause (1) of subsection (b), the Commissioner may base such information upon a sampling of data available from State agencies, including the State educational agencies, and local educational agencies.

"(d)(1) Not later than one hundred twenty days after the close of each fiscal year, the Commissioner shall transmit to the appropriate committees of each House of the Congress a report on the progress being made toward the provision of free appropriate public education to all handicapped children, including a detailed description of all evaluation activities conducted under subsection (b).

"(2) The Commissioner shall include in each such report—

"(A) an analysis and evaluation of the effectiveness of procedures undertaken by each State educational agency, local educational agency, and intermediate educational unit to assure that handicapped children receive special education and related services in the least restrictive environment commensurate with their needs and to improve programs of instruction for handicapped children in day or residential facilities;

"(B) any recommendations for change in the provisions of this part, or any other Federal law providing support for the education of handicapped children; and

"(C) an evaluation of the effectiveness of the procedures undertaken by each such agency or unit to prevent erroneous classification of children as eligible to be counted under section 611, including actions undertaken by the Commissioner to carry out provisions of this Act relating to such erroneous classification.

In order to carry out such analyses and evaluations, the Commissioner shall conduct a statistically valid survey for assessing the effectiveness of individualized educational programs.

"(e) There are authorized to be appropriated for each fiscal year such sums as may be necessary to carry out the provisions of this section. *Appropriation authorization.*

"INCENTIVE GRANTS"

"SEC. 619. (a) The Commissioner shall make a grant to any State which— *20 USC 1419.*

"(1) has met the eligibility requirements of section 612;

"(2) has a State plan approved under section 613; and

"(3) provides special education and related services to handicapped children aged three to five, inclusive, who are counted for the purposes of section 611(a)(1)(A).

The maximum amount of the grant for each fiscal year which a State may receive under this section shall be $300 for each such child in that State.

"(b) Each State which—

"(1) has met the eligibility requirements of section 612,

"(2) has a State plan approved under section 613, and

"(3) desires to receive a grant under this section,

shall make an application to the Commissioner at such time, in such manner, and containing or accompanied by such information, as the Commissioner may reasonably require.

"(c) The Commissioner shall pay to each State having an application approved under subsection (b) of this section the amount to which the State is entitled under this section, which amount shall be used for the purpose of providing the services specified in clause (3) of subsection (a) of this section.

"(d) If the sums appropriated for any fiscal year for making payments to States under this section are not sufficient to pay in full the maximum amounts which all States may receive under this part for such fiscal year, the maximum amounts which all States may receive under this part for such fiscal year shall be ratably reduced. In case additional funds become available for making such payments for any fiscal year during which the preceding sentence is applicable, such reduced amounts shall be increased on the same basis as they were reduced.

"(e) In addition to the sums necessary to pay the entitlements under section 611, there are authorized to be appropriated for each fiscal year such sums as may be necessary to carry out the provisions of this section. *Appropriation authorization.*

"PAYMENTS"

"SEC. 620. (a) The Commissioner shall make payments to each State in amounts which the State educational agency of such State is eligible to receive under this part. Any State educational agency receiving payments under this subsection shall distribute payments *20 USC 1420.*

to the local educational agencies and intermediate educational units of such State in amounts which such agencies and units are eligible to receive under this part after the State educational agency has approved applications of such agencies or units for payments in accordance with section 614(b).

"(b) Payments under this part may be made in advance or by way of reimbursement and in such installments as the Commissioner may determine necessary.".

Regulations. 20 USC 1411 note.

(b)(1) The Commissioner of Education shall, no later than one year after the effective date of this subsection, prescribe—

    (A) regulations which establish specific criteria for determining whether a particular disorder or condition may be considered a specific learning disability for purposes of designating children with specific learning disabilities;

    (B) regulations which establish and describe diagnostic procedures which shall be used in determining whether a particular child has a disorder or condition which places such child in the category of children with specific learning disabilities; and

    (C) regulations which establish monitoring procedures which will be used to determine if State educational agencies, local educational agencies, and intermediate educational units are complying with the criteria established under clause (A) and clause (B).

Proposed regulation, submittal to congressional committees. Publication in Federal Register.

(2) The Commissioner shall submit any proposed regulation written under paragraph (1) to the Committee on Education and Labor of the House of Representatives and the Committee on Labor and Public Welfare of the Senate, for review and comment by each such committee, at least fifteen days before such regulation is published in the Federal Register.

20 USC 402.

(3) If the Commissioner determines, as a result of the promulgation of regulations under paragraph (1), that changes are necessary in the definition of the term "children with specific learning disabilities", as such term is defined by section 602(15) of the Act, he shall submit recommendations for legislation with respect to such changes to each House of the Congress.

Definitions.

(4) For purposes of this subsection:

    (A) The term "children with specific learning disabilities" means those children who have a disorder in one or more of the basic psychological processes involved in understanding or in using language, spoken or written, which disorder may manifest itself in imperfect ability to listen, think, speak, read, write, spell, or do mathematical calculations. Such disorders include such conditions as perceptual handicaps, brain injury, minimal brain dysfunction, dyslexia, and developmental aphasia. Such term does not include children who have learning problems which are primarily the result of visual, hearing, or motor handicaps, of mental retardation, of emotional disturbance, or environmental, cultural, or economic disadvantage.

    (B) The term "Commissioner" means the Commissioner of Education.

20 USC 1411.

(c) Effective on the date upon which final regulations prescribed by the Commissioner of Education under subsection (b) take effect, the amendment made by subsection (a) is amended, in subparagraph (A) of section 611(a)(5) (as such subparagraph would take effect on the effective date of subsection (a)), by adding "and" at the end of clause (i), by striking out clause (ii), and by redesignating clause (iii) as clause (ii).

AMENDMENTS WITH RESPECT TO EMPLOYMENT OF HANDICAPPED INDIVID-
UALS, REMOVAL OF ARCHITECTURAL BARRIERS, AND MEDIA CENTERS

SEC. 6. (a) Part A of the Act is amended by inserting after section   20 USC 1404.
605 thereof the following new sections:

"EMPLOYMENT OF HANDICAPPED INDIVIDUALS

"SEC. 606. The Secretary shall assure that each recipient of assist-   20 USC 1405.
ance under this Act shall make positive efforts to employ and advance
in employment qualified handicapped individuals in programs assisted
under this Act.

"GRANTS FOR THE REMOVAL OF ARCHITECTURAL BARRIERS

"SEC. 607. (a) Upon application by any State or local educational   20 USC 1406.
agency or intermediate educational unit the Commissioner is authorized to make grants to pay part or all of the cost of altering existing
buildings and equipment in the same manner and to the same extent
as authorized by the Act approved August 12, 1968 (Public Law
90–480), relating to architectural barriers.

"(b) For the purpose of carrying out the provisions of this section,   Appropriation
there are authorized to be appropriated such sums as may be   authorization.
necessary.".

(b) Section 653 of the Act (20 U.S.C. 1453) is amended to read
as follows:

"CENTERS ON EDUCATIONAL MEDIA AND MATERIALS FOR THE HANDICAPPED

"SEC. 653. (a) The Secretary is authorized to enter into agreements
with institutions of higher education, State and local educational
agencies, or other appropriate nonprofit agencies, for the establishment and operation of centers on educational media and materials
for the handicapped, which together will provide a comprehensive
program of activities to facilitate the use of new educational tech-
nology in education programs for handicapped persons, including
designing, developing, and adapting instructional materials, and such
other activities consistent with the purposes of this part as the Secretary may prescribe in such agreements. Any such agreement shall—
    "(1) provide that Federal funds paid to a center will be used
solely for such purposes as are set forth in the agreement; and
    "(2) authorize the center involved, subject to prior approval
by the Secretary, to contract with public and private agencies and
organizations for demonstration projects.
"(b) In considering proposals to enter into agreements under this
section, the Secretary shall give preference to institutions and
agencies—
    "(1) which have demonstrated the capabilities necessary for the
development and evaluation of educational media for the handicapped; and
    "(2) which can serve the educational technology needs of the
Model High School for the Deaf (established under Public Law   80 Stat. 1027.
89–694).   Report to
"(c) The Secretary shall make an annual report on activities carried   Congress.
out under this section which shall be transmitted to the Congress.".

Pub. Law 94-142   - 24 -   November 29, 1975

CONGRESSIONAL DISAPPROVAL OF REGULATIONS

SEC. 7. (a)(1) Section 431(d)(1) of the General Education Provisions Act (20 U.S.C. 1232(d)(1)) is amended by inserting "final" immediately before "standard" each place it appears therein.

(2) The third sentence of section 431(d)(2) of such Act (20 U.S.C. 1232(d)(2)) is amended by striking out "proposed" and inserting in lieu thereof "final".

(3) The fourth and last sentences of section 431(d)(2) of such Act (20 U.S.C. 1232(d)(2)) each are amended by inserting "final" immediately before "standard".

(b) Section 431(d)(1) of the General Education Provisions Act (20 U.S.C. 1232(d)(1)) is amended by adding at the end thereof the following new sentence: "Failure of the Congress to adopt such a concurrent resolution with respect to any such final standard, rule, regulation, or requirement prescribed under any such Act, shall not represent, with respect to such final standard, rule, regulation, or requirement, an approval or finding of consistency with the Act from which it derives its authority for any purpose, nor shall such failure to adopt a concurrent resolution be construed as evidence of an approval or finding of consistency necessary to establish a prima facie case, or an inference or presumption, in any judicial proceeding.".

EFFECTIVE DATES

20 USC 1411
note.

SEC. 8. (a) Notwithstanding any other provision of law, the amendments made by sections 2(a), 2(b), and 2(c) shall take effect on July 1, 1975.

(b) The amendments made by sections 2(d), 2(e), 3, 6, and 7 shall take effect on the date of the enactment of this Act.

(c) The amendments made by sections 4 and 5(a) shall take effect on October 1, 1977, except that the provisions of clauses (A), (C), (D), and (E) of paragraph (2) of section 612 of the Act, as amended by this Act, section 617(a)(1)(D) of the Act, as amended by this Act, section 617(b) of the Act, as amended by this Act, and section 618(a) of the Act, as amended by this Act, shall take effect on the date of the enactment of this Act.

(d) The provisions of section 5(b) shall take effect on the date of the enactment of this Act.

Approved November 29, 1975.

LEGISLATIVE HISTORY:

HOUSE REPORTS: No. 94-332 accompanying H.R. 7217 (Comm. on Education and Labor) and 94-664 (Comm. of Conference).
SENATE REPORTS: No. 94-168 (Comm. on Labor and Public Welfare) and No. 94-455 (Comm. of Conference).
CONGRESSIONAL RECORD, Vol. 121 (1975):
    June 18, considered and passed Senate.
    July 21, 29, considered and passed House, amended, in lieu of H.R. 7217.
    Nov. 18, House agreed to conference report.
    Nov. 19, Senate agreed to conference report.
WEEKLY COMPILATION OF PRESIDENTIAL DOCUMENTS, Vol. 11, No. 49:
    Dec. 2, Presidential statement.